I have traveled with L on many of her Deliverance Evangelistic Missions to the nations. We have traveled to Guyana, South America, the Caribbean, St. Vincent, and the Grenadines, Asia, Philippines, the continent of Africa, and North America.

In these nations God has used her to teach and train individuals, leaders, groups, and organization to pull down satanic strongholds and set the captives free. Before she goes to the nations, the Lord gives her a specific prophetic word for the nations. As she conveys the message it is always confirmed by the leader of the churches or someone working within the government.

The prophetic word she presents would help to avert some disaster through prayer and give answers to many questions, bring deliverance, and destroy the stronghold of the enemy in relationships, and between congregational members.

In one particular church in Guyana a complete congregation was held hostage by the spirit of anger. This had caused a division in the church unknowing to Dr. Pauline Walley-Daniels. Through the word of knowledge and wisdom, God addressed the source of the problem being the spirit of anger. The congregation was then able to openly discuss the problem as they identified where blame was laid, causing resentment and disunity.

Through an open forum everyone was able to express their hurt, and a revival of deliverance, reconciliation, and restoration was experienced. God released total healing to an entire church.

This is only a small testimony of the work done through the Prophetic Deliverance Ministry of Dr. Pauline Walley-Daniels. Indeed God is using her through training, equipping and empowering to pull down satanic strongholds and to build godly strongmen and strongwomen to advance the kingdom of God.

—EVANGELIST RENNA JOSEPH
OVERCOMERS' HOUSE
BRONX, NEW YORK

I write to note that I have known and have been associated with Dr. Walley-Daniels since 1998. I first met her at a prayer meeting organized by a common acquaintance, and because of the authenticity I felt about her calling, I became associated with her ministry. At the time I met her, the area of deliverance ministration was quite foreign to me though I had been a Christian for many years. Over the years, I have watched her minister to many and have also benefited from her ministrations. I can therefore state without any equivocation that her calling is in the area of prophetic deliverance ministration. To carry out this mandate, she routinely functions in the gifts of discerning of spirits, word of knowledge, and word of wisdom. I have no doubt that the Lord has called her as a prophet to the nations to help set His people free.

—DR. STEPHEN U. AJA
BROOKLYN COLLEGE OF THE CITY UNIVERSITY
OF NEW YORK
BROOKLYN, NEW YORK

I truly recommend Dr. Pauline Walley-Daniels as a five-fold ministry gift to the body of Christ. Walking in both the evangelistic and prophetic offices, with much integrity, honor, and power, her book on prophetic deliverance is an empowerment to the body of Christ, especially to ministers.

—PASTOR J.E.S. PHILLIP
NEWARK, NEW JERSEY

I became a part of the Pauline Walley Evangelistic Ministries in 1998 through an old associate of mine, who introduced me to the ministry. Since then I have had the privilege of seeing Dr. Pauline minister, and I have also seen the instant manifestation of God's Word.

Around 1999 I met Bro. Henry to whom Dr. Pauline gave a word of Revelation during a ministration. She told him she saw where there was a witchcraft attack that had become a blockage to his life's progress and had also become a physical blockage to his health. She told him that if he were to feed on the Word for three months that God would cause him to pass it out and it would change his life forever. Bro. Henry followed the instruction and at the end of the three months, he came running into the office saying, "I just passed it out, I felt a weight lifted when it went out." Bro. Henry described the substance as a black ball like a creature that seemed to have hair and teeth, and it was ugly. He said he would have carried it for us to see but he was afraid. Dr. Pauline had travelled at the time when he passed it out; he left New York before Dr. Pauline returned from her mission to Asia. Soon after, he wrote from Ohio to tell us he got a job, bought a home and a car, and was doing well.

Also, there was a night we were in ministration when a sister called the ministry and Dr. Pauline told her to come in. As soon as she entered, Dr. Pauline started rebuking the spirit of death. Then the lady fainted and literally died before us. There was no pulse or breath in her. Dr. Pauline then asked us all to begin to speak in tongues so that we would be in one accord. She also asked us to plead the blood against the spirit of death. She then began calling the lady's name, commanding her Sister Victoria to come forth; the sister began to cough and sneeze, then they sat her up. When Sister Victoria came around, she asked what happened because she felt that something strange had happened to her. Dr. Pauline then sent for an ambulance to take her to the doctor for evaluation; the doctor certified that she was all right.

—REV. ALTHIA ROWE
OVERCOMERS' HOUSE
BRONX, NEW YORK

I first met Dr. Pauline in Guyana, February 2008, at a School of Deliverance Conference. I was particularly impressed with her humility and trust in God. I observed that she was a woman of God, ordained by God for this time. Her ministry captivated me; there was an impartation of anointing and knowledge. I was open to receive from the woman of God. I know this was my divine encounter, and God placed Dr.

Pauline in my life so that I could fulfill my destiny and purpose in God.

After my deliverance training I was empowered to move on. I was a part of a ministry where God was using me in the prophetic, but I was boxed-up and limited. There was not much freedom and I was prepared to take it like that and live with it. I thought that was a sign of humility and willingness to continue in that fashion. But Dr. Pauline helped me to understand my calling and work, doing the will of God, and having the fruit of the Spirit manifest in my life.

After which I then was very happy doing the will of God, never minding the circumstances. She left a Godly impression on me. I was determined to get more from the woman of God, so wherever I knew she was going to minister, if it was possible I went. In May, 2008, I came to New York for the Divine Encounter Conference; while there I really had a divine encounter with God. She prophesied to me, she is authentic; God really speaks to her and directs her.

I mean things that God had spoken to me about my ministry work and purpose in God; she spoke of and awakened the hunger I had in me. I returned home to St. Martin a new person, being unraveled and free in the Spirit to do the will of God.

God has placed Dr. Pauline in my life as my mentor, and a good thing about her is that she always teaches forgiveness and Holy living and whenever a problem arrives or the enemy tries to obstruct me in any way, I always hear her voice, as though I was still in the School of Deliverance. Dr. Pauline and her ministry have played a great part in my spiritual life and in me and allowing me to fulfill my destiny and purpose in God in six months.

—PASTOR JOAN IRELAND
ANGELIC TOUCH MINISTRY INTERNATIONAL
ST. MARTIN, WEST INDIES

# SCHOOL *of* PROPHETIC *Deliverance*

*Pauline*
WALLEY-DANIELS, PhD

CREATION
HOUSE
A STRANG COMPANY

SCHOOL OF PROPHETIC DELIVERANCE
by Pauline Walley-Daniels
Published by Creation House
A Strang Company
600 Rinehart Road
Lake Mary, Florida 32746
www.creationhouse.com

Unless otherwise noted, all Scripture quotations are from the New King James Version of the Bible. Copyright © 1979, 1980, 1982 by Thomas Nelson, Inc., publishers. Used by permission.

Scripture quotations marked KJV are from the King James Version of the Bible.

Cover design by Amanda Potter

Library of Congress Control Number: 2008939238
International Standard Book Number: 978-1-59979-548-5

First Edition

08 09 10 11 12 — 987654321
Printed in the United States of America

# ACKNOWLEDGMENTS

S PECIAL THANKS TO the Almighty God, who has put in me the spirit of humility to receive teaching and counseling through the power of the Holy Spirit.

Thanks to my parents, Bishop Enoch and Felicia Walley, and other members of my family for bringing me up in the fear of God.

I hereby express my profound appreciation to the individuals who have stood with me at Overcomers' House and have encouraged me through my valleys and mountains with Pauline Walley Evangelistic Ministries. These include our partners, supporters, organizers, coordinators, and all who are affiliated to Pauline Walley Ministries known as Overcomers around the world.

Special thanks to our coordinators in Europe, Africa, Caribbean, Asia, and America for coming on board to support this unique work around the world. I wish I could include all the names of my special loved ones, supporters, and international coordinators, but time and space will not permit me to do so. However, I give thanks to all those who have contributed to the progressiveness of my life and ministry.

Special thanks to my unique editor, Kay Coulter, whose work and advice have been very inspiring and encouraging to me. My appreciation also goes to the father of prophets, Bishop Bill Hamon of Christian International, for ordaining me and validating my work and ministry.

Finally, it is good to be married; a special thank you to my beloved husband, Pastor Frederick R. Daniels, who has been a great support and enhancement to my life and ministry.

# CONTENTS

# FOREWORD

I N THIS BOOK Dr. Pauline Walley covers a subject very near to my heart. I have functioned as a prophet in the body of Christ for more than fifty years. We have pioneered and fathered the prophetic movement since it was birthed into the church world in 1988.

I carefully read this manuscript before I wrote the Foreword. I can honestly say that Dr. Pauline has properly presented biblical truth concerning the prophets. Her explanation of prophetic revelation, language, deliverance, and how to administrate the prophetic is true and workable. Dr. Pauline has a zeal, as I do, for the integrity, righteousness, and accuracy of prophets and prophetic ministry.

Every one that wants to properly minister in prophetic ministry needs to read and study the principles presented in this book. God bless you, Dr. Pauline, for having the heart of God and mind of Christ for His prophets and prophetic ministry.

—DR. BILL HAMON
Bishop of Christian International Ministries Network
Author of Seven Major Books: *The Eternal Church,*
*Prophets and Personal Prophecy,*
*Prophets and the Prophetic Movement,*
*Prophets, Pitfalls and Principles*
*Apostles, Prophets and the Coming Moves of God*
*The Day of the Saints*
*Who Am I and Why Am I Here?*

# PREFACE

D R. PAULINE WALLEY-DANIELS is strongly gifted in several areas of the prophetic. She ministers prophetic deliverance. The Word of the Lord through her propels people into their destiny; brings understanding, healing, and enlightenment; pulls down satanic strongholds; and releases the love and joy of the Lord.

Her prophetic gift and anointing flow out of a life immersed in intercession and warfare prayers and discipline. The information is very accurate, sometimes with God confirming His Word with signs following within twenty-four hours.

The Lord has been using her to speak prophetically over nations, leaders of nations, bishops, apostles, and business leaders, owners, and CEO's. She prays prophetically over children, youth, marriages, and businesses.

Her prophetic teaching is filled with nuggets and pearls. At this time in the history of the world, leaders are looking for solutions to complex problems. The church is faced with issues never before seen or heard of. The whole earth groans for the manifestation of the sons of God. One of the five-fold gifts to the church to bring these sons to maturity is the prophet.

This book is a tool to be added to the arsenal or ammunition already written bringing prophetic change and direction to all who will read it. These pages are the result of years of experience. As we travel to nations, I have witnessed changes as Dr. Pauline operates under a mandate to bring deliverance.

I recommend this book to you. As you use it to read and teach, you will experience change in your life, ministry, family, and nation. Your life will never be the same. Receive fresh vision, new beginnings, and restoration.

—REV. YVONNE RICHARDS
INTERNATIONAL CHRISTIAN LEADERSHIP CONNECTION,
NEW YORK

# INTRODUCTION

## My Ministerial Treasure

One of the most interesting gifts that I have treasured in my life is the insight into the prophetic realms. The prophetic office is a ministerial treasure. The ability to hear from the Lord and to deliver accurately His prophetic word according to time and season can be very exciting.

Also, the ability to understand prophetic interpretation is awesome, and I bless God for this unique gifting that has been a source of strength in my relationship with the Lord Jesus Christ. The prophetic ministry has been a great enhancement to my ministry around the world.

Without the prophetic gift, it is not easy to minister deliverance to people. A deep insight into the prophetic realms enables me to listen and follow divine instructions when pulling down satanic strongholds. To God be the glory; great things He has done. Amen!

In the summer of 2006, I had just returned from a mission trip to five nations in West Africa (Republic of

Benin, Togo, Sierra Leone, Liberia, and Ghana) and was trying to catch up on my rest, when I had an intuition to go on a three-day fast. Although I needed a rest, I proceeded by asking all Overcomers (my team members at Overcomers' House) to join me in the fast.

When I announced the fast, everyone was surprised because they had been fasting to support my trip and were just concluding the fast on my return. I then persuaded them with an explanation that it was a divine mandate. Surprisingly, both adults and children aged six to fifteen years participated in the fast.

On the afternoon of the first day of the fast, July 25, 2006, I was sitting in my office at Overcomers' House when I heard a voice saying, "Prepare a note for the School of Prophets that the people may understand what you are going to teach." Immediately, I pulled out my teaching notes from my computer desktop and began to write. A unique inspiration came over me, and by the end of that day, I had completed five pages. By the end of the week, I was ready with Volume I of the manuscript.

This book, *Prophetic Deliverance and the Prophetic Language,* is based on the foundational knowledge that every Christian needs in order to understand the difference between the inspirational gift of prophecy and the office of the prophet. Many people do not know the difference, and they think that anyone exercising an inspirational gift is a prophet. Hence, many have been misled and some are hurt and disappointed.

There are different types of prophets. Some are called

and chosen, some are adopted, and others are assumed. The self-appointed prophets try to control and manipulate situations into being. Those who trust in the vessel other than the Creator need education, otherwise they will always be hurt by the vessel on which they depend.

Beloved, knowledge is power; education is wisdom. This book will turn your life around. Stay blessed and enjoy His unique presence as you read this book.

# Chapter 1

# UNDERSTANDING THE OFFICE OF THE PROPHET

WHEN I WAS growing up, the prophetic ministry was not popular in the mainstream churches. The Orthodox, the Protestants, and the Evangelicals were all skeptical about the prophetic. Although some churchgoers would sneak in and out of "prayer houses" where spiritism was practiced to seek clairvoyants and spiritual direction, those same churchgoers would openly deny the office of the prophet in the church.

Matters regarding sicknesses, diseases, mishaps, misfortunes, and thefts, among other problems, often lured people to seek both the prophet and the spiritualist outside the regular church relationship and environment. Some individuals involved in business transactions at various levels would consult a prophet or spiritualist for spiritual guidance and direction. Churchgoers would often travel far away from their homes and neighborhoods to seek prophetic or spiritual attention.

During my childhood school days, some children would suddenly disappear from school for days or weeks to engage in some ritual following a prophetic or spiritual utterance spoken over their lives. Some of the rituals that were prescribed for these children were with regards to protection. Whenever these categories of children reappeared in school, they returned with new sets of jewelry (necklaces, earrings, bracelets, and rings) with the symbol of the crucifix embedded on them.

The wearing of the crucifix and other spiritual ornaments was very common during examination periods. Some hid the ornament under their garments while some showed it off. Some even appeared with recitation from certain "prayer books" and "masters" as well as from the book of Psalms. Interestingly, our parents warned us not to mingle with children who wore spiritual ornaments. Some of the children that wore spiritual artifices were considered dangerous and weird because their parents indulged in diabolic activities by consulting or practicing magic and spiritualism.

For instance, it was a common thing for writing materials like pens, pencils, and erasers to be tossed or stolen among school children. There were physical fights and bullying among children who had the habit of taking things that did not belong to them. While teachers sought wise methods to control funny habits among school children, some parents took the matter too far by consulting clairvoyants and even bring harm to other children over petty behaviors. Hence, some children suffered mysterious interferences with their health and progress in life.

The prophetic ministry has been practiced righteously by those who know the truth and wrongfully by those who are ignorant. The truth is that mankind is created in God's own image; therefore, there is a part of mankind that is connected to the spiritual realm (Gen. 1:26). The part of mankind that is connected to the spiritual realm wants to know the mind of God and to respond to the will of God as it is in heaven. "Thy will be done in earth, as it is in heaven" (Matt. 6:10, KJV).

Both the righteous and the ungodly claim an identity and a sense of belonging to God. People of different faiths and beliefs all claim a sense of belonging to the Creator of heaven and earth. Even Satan himself holds a claim of belonging to God.

The part of man that seeks identification and recognition with God motivates a person to search for God and His divine will through whatever spiritual avenue that is available. The source of spirituality that is available may be right or wrong or even corrupted. As a result, the desire to be closer to God could lead to some sort of entanglement to error.

Human beings have a strong desire to hear from the Creator and to be connected to Him directly or indirectly.

The quest for divine connection calls for an attention to the prophetic ministry. The prophetic ministry is highly desired and welcomed, unfortunately even when the vessel is not living up to our community or environmental standards. Yet because of the connection to the heavenly realms, we are prone to tilt towards the voice of God without much attention to the instrument involved.

Although many powerful books have been written on the subject of the prophetic, there is knowledge that comes and with it a season to support or upgrade the existing information. Having been involved in both the prophetic and deliverance ministry for about thirty years, I felt the need to focus on the importance of prophetic deliverance, which is the core of my evangelistic ministry.

Also, following a divine direction, I was compelled to respond to the need for this message at this time. Many of the people that come to us for deliverance ministration do not often speak out their problems. Their approach is, "I hear you are a prophet, so you should be able to tackle my problems without me telling you anything." In fact, some of our guests will not even provide an iota of information for us to work with. We often depend on "a word of knowledge, a word of wisdom, and discerning of spirits" to solve problems and to minister to people. Above all, we focus our ministration on the Word of God to minister from a scriptural perspective.

Some people are ignorant of their own problems, while some are too secretive to expose the work of the enemy. They would rather keep the devil in their closets than expose him to the blood of Jesus Christ flowing from the cross of Calvary.

## My Prophetic Encounter

When I was very young I used to see and say stuff that sounded strange and weird. Both of my parents and people around me did not understand some of the things I said or why I made those statements, because we were all ignorant. The things I saw were spiritual and were taught to be things that should only be seen by adults—especially elderly persons. The statements I made that were based on what I saw were considered to be too heavy for a child to say. It was assumed that I must have been listening to adults' conversations or I was being too forward and nosy. My people did not realize that God's hands were upon me, and my mission on earth was being manifested.

> Before I formed you in the womb I knew you; Before you were born I sanctified you; I ordained you a prophet to the nations.
> —JEREMIAH 1:5, NKJV

Meanwhile, I was having unique experiences and seeing visions of angels and hearing a voice speaking to me. I would usually fall into a trance and see events happening as though I was in a movie theatre watching a film or a drama on stage.

During my early childhood, my parents were part of the Jehovah's Witness movement, so we had no direct contact with Pentecostal churches. Hence, I knew nothing about visions or revelations. Although I was having divine encounters, I did not know the meaning of my experiences. However, I had a great desire to go to a Pentecostal church.

There were some Pentecostal churches in our neighborhood where spiritual gifts were openly demonstrated. I would sneak out into their services and watch them sing and dance. Yet I did not understand what their performances were all about.

One day, at about the age of eight or nine, I had a vision while I was sitting in class. My seat was by the window, and I saw a ladder that went from earth to heaven on the school compound. I saw a huge "being" seated on the top of the ladder with his hand stretched out beckoning me to come to him. So I began to climb up the ladder and the vision disappeared. From that moment my heart began to desire the things of God. A hunger for righteousness began to develop in me.

Another time in class, I fell into a trance. This time I saw the Lord Jesus Christ come to my school compound. All of the children from all of the schools in the neighborhood began to run out of their classrooms to meet with Him. They were hopping and jumping into the arms of Jesus. There were multitudes of children, yet when I got there, Jesus pointed his hand, beckoned to me, and said, "I have come for you." Suddenly the vision disappeared.

Soon after that encounter, my dad employed a private teacher to tutor me after school. I would tell my teacher my vision in a form of a story. Then the teacher would illustrate my narration in the form of a picture on the board and relate it to a Bible story. One day the teacher told my dad that he would add Bible studies to my subjects and he agreed. I was very happy because this gave me joy and hope that the Lord would one day visit me physically as I had seen in my vision.

Later I saw myself wearing white and standing before a huge crowd, while a unique being was seated in a cloud dictating things for me to present to the people. I would usually see things happening as though I was watching television, and those things would also come to pass in reality. Today that vision is in reality my life and ministry. Revelations still come to me in the form of movies both during teaching ministration and the writing of my books.

During my teenage days, one of my aunties, Auntie Susan, took us to a Presbyterian church. The service was rigid and the preaching was a story telling activity. Every Sunday, the greatest part of the service was dedicated to choir rendition and singing groups' performances. Although the Bible was read, the sermon was a story telling exhortation told over and over, which did not carry an evangelistic message. Meanwhile, my desire to meet with the Lord increased from deep within. I started reading the Bible on my own because I wanted to be a spokesperson for God.

When I went to high school, I got into trouble with my mouth several times within a week. I was talking too much, telling people what I saw about them. The revelations were vivid and detailed. I was not diplomatic and did not attempt to hide anything.

Since everybody was ignorant and no one knew the intricacies of the prophetic manifestations and the power of God that was operating in me, people began to call me a "witch" because they thought only witches had the ability to discern beyond the ordinary. Many of my mates disliked me because my prophetic gifts enabled me to reveal secrets of issues that were kept hidden. At one point the whole school was afraid of my prophetic utterances, hence they turned against me, and everyone was told not to relate to me because I would reveal secrets.

> But the LORD said to me: "Do not say, 'I am a youth,' For you shall go to all to whom I send you, And whatever I command you, you shall speak. Do not be afraid of their faces, For I am with you to deliver you, says the LORD.
> —JEREMIAH 1:7–8

When we returned from one semester break, I got into deeper trouble as I was able to tell who did what at home during the holidays. I tried to warn people to avoid doing certain things and to tell them what the results would be if they should go ahead with them. I also confronted some of our mates who had sexual affairs and committed abortions, and all hell broke loose.

Fortunately, the Lord intervened and turned my situation around. One morning during breakfast in the school dining hall, one senior student came over to my table and held me up, then announced, "This is Holy Virgin Mary. Let anyone who has never sinned cast a stone at her." All the male students stood up and began to hail me as "Holy Virgin Mary," while they mocked at the girls that sat around their tables. From that moment onward, my name changed from being called a "witch" to "Holy Virgin Mary." That was the beginning of a great deliverance for me and also the beginning of respect and acceptance of my prophetic ministry among my schoolmates.

From then on fellow students came to make inquiries and to ask for prayers. When someone was sick, they laid the person on my bed or asked me to bless water for their healing. Most female students would not relate to me unless they were in need.

One day the Lord decided to confirm my ministry openly when He visited me during lecture hours. It was about 9:00 a.m., just before the school dismissed for breakfast. All classes were in session. But unexpectedly, the teacher in our class gave us an early break and most of the students in my classroom left. I could not move as I had entered into a realm which I didn't understand and my whole body was trembling and my mouth was numb.

Everywhere was quiet. Then suddenly I felt a unique Presence that engulfed me and left me suspended in the air. I felt the whole world was spinning while it looked cloudy everywhere. Spontaneously I began to speak out in tongues, which practice I had never heard or known before except for reading it in Scripture. The students ran out of their classrooms and came running towards me. Some of them began to exclaim, "Jesus has come to visit the holy Mary!" These and many more experiences drew me closer to God and gave me the confidence to stay more in His presence from then until now.

The mistakes I made and the challenges I faced when I did not know what I was seeing or saying had been good training ground for me. The experience from my trials and temptations drew me closer to God, while it took me to the school of the Holy Spirit to learn endurance, tolerance, patience, understanding, and maturity.

Romans 5:3–5 tells us:

> And not only that, but we also glory in tribulations, knowing that tribulation produces perseverance; and perseverance, character; and character, hope. Now hope does not disappoint, because the love of God has been poured out in our hearts by the Holy Spirit who was given to us.

I have done a lot of studies and read many books to prod myself to handle this ministry with maturity. Today I know how to keep my mouth shut, and even if I know everything about a person at first sight, I will not speak until the Lord urges me to do so. When people insist and persuade me to speak the Word of the Lord, I tell them I am in prophetic deliverance and I will not speak until the Lord has set the solution before me. I do not touch any assignment that God has not given me grace to perform. We need a measure of grace to carry the burdens that people turn over to us. We need a special grace to get involved in certain situations; otherwise we will be hurt by the trials and temptations that come with every assignment. The prophetic ministry is sensitive and delicate. The essence of this book is to help people who depend heavily on the prophetic word to understand the essence of the prophetic word and its interpretations.

# The Prophet

A prophet is one who speaks for God or a deity. A prophet is a person chosen to speak for God, to lead, to direct, to instruct, or to guide a people or a nation. A prophet is one who stays constantly in the presence of God to receive His divine will for the people in time and season. The prophet delivers the Word of the Lord as it is, without interfering with the contents of the message.

A true prophet of God does not interfere with the meaning of the message received but delivers it as is in order not to encounter the wrath of God due to misinterpretation. Thus a prophet who has the fear of God in his or her behavior and character will be careful of his or her utterances.

A prophet may mislead a people when he or she attempts to interfere with the contents of the message received by giving an interpretation which may be correct or incorrect. An attempt to present the interpretation instead of delivering the exact message received usually corrupts the prophetic word (Gen. 2:16–18; 3:1–3).

A true prophet is one who exercises the fear of God even in delivering the word received and who is careful not to mingle the message with the interpretation unless he or she is divinely instructed to do so. Once a prophetic word is distorted, even a true prophet will be delivering a false message to the people concerned. Where there is a gift of interpretation, a true prophet will usually differentiate the original message from the interpretation that follows. A true prophet will also distinguish between that which the Lord has spoken or revealed and that which comes from his or her own personal understanding.

## The Distorted Message and Misinterpretation

A false prophet is one who, although hearing or receiving from God, usually presents a distorted message to the people concerned by trying to interfere with the contents of the message through interpretation that may either be correct or incorrect. Usually a prophet who interferes with the content of the prophetic word does not state exactly what is received. That prophet will only give out the interpretation of what he or she thinks the context is about.

The approach of assuming the interpretation of a prophetic word is dangerous because the recipient does not get to hear the main revelation, but only a distorted message that could be confusing and deceptive. In the process of interpretation, the prophet may add or subtract from it (Rev. 22:19).

Sometimes our personal interest in a matter or our

desire for favor can inject selfish expressions into the prophetic message during delivery. Sometimes a false burden or display of power in order to get personal attention can motivate a person to manipulate prophetic delivery and interpretation instead of taking a Christ-centered approach. In the passage from Jesus' temptation, the enemy tried to distort the Word of God, but Jesus stayed focused and thwarted his evil plans (Matt. 4:1–11).

Like the postmaster who has no authority to interfere with the letters meant for delivery, except on rare occasions as permitted by law, a prophet is not supposed to interfere with the original word received from God. It is forbidden to break the seal of a parcel that is not meant for you but merely for delivery to another person. By governmental law, anyone who interferes with a parcel meant for delivery to a client is liable for punishment of either fine or imprisonment or both.

Many people do not understand the intricacies of delivering a distorted message, nor do they know that interfering with the content is a sin. The practice of wanting to show off one's prophetic prowess in public and to attract public attention to one's ability is becoming rampant. Some people can hardly study their Bibles or sit in their local church Bible studies for more than an hour, yet they want to declare themselves as prophets to the public.

A true prophet spends quality time daily in the presence of God. A true prophet does not speak until the Lord has commanded him or her to do so. When a true prophet opens up his or her mouth, it sounds like a trumpet from heaven or smells like fresh bread from the baker's oven. There are those who may not be false prophets but are prone to delivering false messages because they often concern themselves with the interpretation of the messages instead of presenting the original word.

In recent times, in the midst of seeking acceptance there are people who edit the contents of a prophetic word in order not to offend the recipients. In the process of editing, colorful language has been applied which often distorts the meaning and interpretation of the word. Sometimes a prophetic word needs to be rugged and unusual in order for it to make an impact in the life of the recipient.

# Definition of Related Terms

### Prophecy

A word of prophecy is a divinely inspired statement or revelation of what is to come. A word of prophecy describes a type of revelation that is made instantly by the power of the spoken word. It is a statement, a question, a direction, an instruction, or guidance that is ordained and purposed without human influence or innovation.

### Prophesy

To prophesy is the state of uttering a divinely inspired revelation. Prophesying is the process of releasing an utterance that is coming directly from the throne of God. It is the state of the action, where a person flows with a unique eloquence that has a supernatural influence and demonstration.

## Prophetic

To be prophetic involves an action, utterance, or writing that is related to a divinely inspired statement. A prophetic action demonstrates divine revelation—a prophetic word. This word of revelation is either predictive or it can be a performance that carries the omen of prophetic functions.

# Who Is a Prophet?

There are various functions that describe a person as a prophet. The individuals that operate in the office of the prophet also consider themselves to be close to the Almighty God through various means. Hence, they demonstrate a sense of belonging that tags them as being special, some even behaving like Nazarites to differentiate themselves from other people. An individual involved in the prophetic ministry usually considers his or herself as a child of God, a spokesperson for God, a servant of God, and a friend of God.

## A child of God

A prophet is a child of God. He or she is a person who sees God as his or her father. Like a child, he or she sits and listens to God as a child would to his or her father. A father-son or father-daughter relationship is very crucial in order to feel the heart of God and to understand what He says. A son understands the father beyond his utterances, he takes note of the father's actions and countenance as well as his moves, and the son responds accordingly.

The action of a father sometimes speaks louder than the expression of words. A child has an exceptional relationship with his father. A child sits on the lap of his father. Jesus is described as the Son of God, so He was able to convey the heart of God to mankind. John the Beloved sat at the bosom of the Lord Jesus Christ, so he was able to see the heart of the Father, enabling him to write the book of Revelation, the Gospel of John, and the epistles of John.

### A spokesman or woman of God

A prophet is a representative of God. He or she is an ambassador that utters the mind of God. He or she takes notes from God and presents the message to the people as it is. He or she is a person that occupies the prophetic office to represent the interest of God. He or she mediates between God and the people. A prophet's focus is to let the people know what God is saying or what God expects of the people.

Moses was a spokesman who represented God before Pharaoh. Moses went back and forth between God and Pharaoh and did exactly what God commanded him to do (Exod. 5:1–3). A spokesman or woman sits at the feet of the Master. Moses was a spokesman who sat at the feet of God to receive divine instruction to deliver the children of Israel from the house of bondage, and he also received the Ten Commandments for Israel (Exod. 19:8–9, 20:1–17).

**A servant of God**

A servant is a person who has been employed to serve his master faithfully and dedicatedly in a high capacity. A servant of God is a prophet who has been dedicated to carry the word or voice of God to a people. A servant does not change or add to the message. A servant just delivers the message at hand. A servant is strictly an errand boy or girl.

Samuel was a servant prophet who played the errand role between Jehovah God and Israel. Samuel never did anything on his own but only that which the Lord instructed him to do. He did not interpret a message but delivered the Word of the Lord as it was given to him.

**A friend of God**

A friend is one who is affectionately attached to another with a high level of trust and dedication. The Scripture describes Abraham as a friend of God. Abraham had a dedicated relationship with God, and God trusted Abraham with an everlasting covenant to be carried out throughout the generations of human existence.

A prophet who is a friend is not only a spokesperson but also one who also has an interactive relationship with the Lord. A friendly relationship allows a person to speak on behalf of others and stand in the gap to intercede for other people. Both Abraham and Moses had interactive relationships with God and so could supplicate for others. Abraham supplicated for Lot and the destruction of Sodom and Gomorrah, while Moses on many occasions supplicated for the children of Israel.

# Prophetic Attraction

The prophetic ministry is an attractive assignment that draws the attention of all manner of people. Human beings have a desire to hear the voice of God. Wherever the voice of God is sounding, humans are drawn to listen. However, individuals have the tendency to want to do their own thing which leads to disobedience. Thus, even after God has spoken, many people still want to act upon their personal feelings.

The prophetic word is a persuasive language with a unique appeal that draws humans to God. It gives a sense of belonging to the rejected and acceptance to the lost. Even when the instrument or person being used is not attractive, the prophetic word that is being released is respected and honored.

Humans usually feel accepted and drawn to God when they hear the prophetic voice. Similarly, people who occupy the office of the prophet tend to feel respected among others. Individuals who operate in the prophetic are usually respected and revered because of their relationship with the Most High God.

### Divine connection

Prophecy provides a link between God and man. Both the righteous and the ungodly can be connected to God through the prophetic word. Sinners are attracted and drawn back to God through the prophetic word.

Interestingly, people usually feel connected to God because they have heard a prophetic word or have seen a revelation. Whether a person occupies the office of a prophet or not, people who have the opportunity to demonstrate the revelatory gifting randomly feel more connected to God because they heard the voice of God or they were used to fulfill a unique mission that came to pass.

Divine connection is not a one-time thing. To be divinely connected means a progressive relationship that provides a forum for continuity. The purpose of God is to keep us connected to Himself. When we are not connected, He uses the prophetic word to get our attention and to remind us that He cares and loves us.

**A sense of belonging**

A prophet must have a sense of belonging towards the deity he represents. Otherwise, that prophet will lack confidence and will not feel like a part of the God he represents or the message he carries. That prophet cannot be zealous for God's purpose and desire.

The prophetic word gives people a sense of belonging and a confidence to identify with God. Therefore, a person who claims to be a prophet must have a strong sense of belonging to God in order to reflect a deep knowledge of God.

John 10:27–30 declares:

*My sheep hear My voice, and I know them, and they follow Me.* And I give them eternal life, and they shall never perish; neither shall anyone snatch them out of My hand. My father, who has given them to Me, is greater than all; and no one is able to snatch them out of My Father's hand. *I and My Father are one.*

—EMPHASIS ADDED

## Feeling of relationship

A prophet must have a good feeling of his personal relationship with God. By so doing the prophet will be passionate and will relate with both God and the people from a passionate point of view. Moses had a passionate relationship with God and the people he was sent to deliver.

Often, as soon as people receive the prophetic word, they sense closeness in their relationship with God. Recently a friend who was undergoing a spiritual recovery shared with me a testimony of his relationship with God. According to him, he knows God loves him, because in his seven years of Christianity, God has spoken to him twice. The first experience came as a call in his life to be actively involved in church. The second came to him two years ago when he was in the valley of decision. He said, "I cannot forget that beautiful experience. I felt specially loved and still feel good about it."

I watched my friend quietly as he narrated his divine experience with a unique passion. At one point I noticed that his countenance changed as he made a sober reflection to try and capture a one-time experience with God. He concluded his narration by stating, "I know God loves me, and he is waiting for me to return to active involvement in church."

I admired the aura of sobriety that came over him as he recaptured that lovely encounter with God. Then I said to myself, "What a feeling of belonging?" Although he had heard the voice of God only twice in seven years, the memory of it still makes a lot of impact in his life. I was deeply touched by his testimony.

My friend's testimony gave me a feeling that I am a spoilt child and challenged my spiritual tantrums. I flare up if I do not hear His voice in a week or so. I say, "God, you're not talking to me about this or that and you know your people are expecting me to bring them a word." I will think I have been disobedient and have not followed some instruction, so the Lord has gone quiet on me.

On this day, listening to another person's testimony made a great difference in my life. I began to cherish every moment that the Lord has granted me opportunity to come into His presence beyond just a prayer. I began to appreciate the fact that I have a unique opportunity that most people do not have. I began to appreciate that blessing of being a spokesperson for the Most High God.

Once upon a time I was a happy little girl that giggled with laughter. I would sit in the presence of the Lord and have a whole day of conversation with Him. I would enjoy interesting scenes that will tickle me to giggle and laugh for hours. I wish I could rewind some of those lovely moments. Although I still enjoy some of those sweet hours, it is not the same as it used to be. My friend's testimony awakened me to return to the mountains to stay in God's presence like never before.

### Feeling of sonship

Although each prophet has a unique relationship with God, people who do not understand the terms of relationship usually assume that every prophet is a son of God.

A son relationship is very personal. A prophet must endeavor to identify the kind of relationship that is entailed in his or her office. A son is not the same as a servant, and a servant is not the same as a spokesman.

# Cherished

It is usually assumed that the prophet does enjoy extra loving care from God. Thus God treats the prophet as a special child or a pet child. Many young prophets do give people that impression. It is not a bad idea to think that a prophet is one of God's pet children. A prophet must feel highly favored among all others just as Mary was described as highly favored among all women (Luke 1:28). However, whether one is a highly favored pet child or not, the fact is that God gives attention to anyone who submits to His authority and walks in obedience.

For a prophet to be adequate, he or she needs to understand the essence of attention, motivation, and encouragement.

## Attention

The prophetic office is attention-seeking and demanding. A prophet needs to give God a good level of attention to be able to fulfill that office effectively. Moses was always in the presence of God. That was why he was able to hear the interpretation and the full details of the Ten Commandments, the basis for the books of the Law in the Old Testament.

When people receive the prophetic word at certain seasons in their lives, they feel very much cherished by God, and they may weep or cry for the joy of being so cherished. Some laugh and their countenances change for good because they heard the prophetic word.

## Motivation

The prophetic word is a great motivation for many people. Sometimes all that is needed in a church service is the prophetic word. Once the prophecy is released, the atmosphere is changed and the people are motivated to worship and praise the Lord.

## Encouragement

The prophetic word is an encouragement to all and sundry. Everyone feels related to God and all want to hear the voice of God. People are encouraged when they hear the voice of God.

# Loved

### Emotional experience

Love is emotional, and people tend to be very emotional when they come into the presence of God. Hence, people weep and cry as they express their feelings before God. The prophetic seems to open up people's emotional dispositions. Both men and women of great caliber are moved to open up their emotions when they hear the voice of God through the prophetic word.

### Emotional attachment

Some people tend to be emotionally attached to the prophetic word because it gives them a sense of belonging. They think that is the only channel through which they can feel the love of God, so they go about seeking the prophetic word all the time.

### Emotional expression

Emotional expression during prophetic ministry includes laughing, crying, weeping, shouting, screaming, singing, dancing, jumping, rolling on the floor, and such. Many people miss God and coming into contact with Him is a unique time of expression that cannot be compared with anything on earth. God is love, and people want to exhibit all manner of expressions to fall into His arms of love.

**Sense of belonging**

When people are allowed to express themselves in the presence of God by exhibiting their emotions, they begin to develop a sense of love and acceptance. They are apt to open up for change; hence they are transformed with passion.

The presence of God is passionate and persuasive. Therefore people should be allowed to feel like babies and little children in the house of the Lord, especially during prophetic ministration.

When a church restricts people from expressing their baby-like emotions, they are not able to experience joy and love that is portrayed in the prophetic. The prophetic usually swings people from the physical body into the spiritual realm so that they may experience the love and touch of the Father.

# A Stirring-up

The prophetic ministry stirs up curiosity. People are curious about what God has to say concerning their daily endeavors and destiny. Whenever human beings sense the presence of the prophetic, one of these things happens:

**Desire to know**

The human mind is besieged with many unanswered questions to which only God can provide answers. People always want to know the mind of God concerning what concerns them either directly or indirectly.

A prophet's ability to know should not be a license to speak when God has not given him or her permission to do so. The desire to know often makes people hang around individual prophets. People operating in the office of the prophet must be careful not to allow their spirits to be used for wrong motives.

## Wishes

The human heart and mind are full of wishes that are either genuine or concocted, yet each person expects God to meet their needs or fulfill their wishes. The prophet is made to feel obligated to draw God's attention to these wishes.

Individuals operating in the prophetic gifts and offices are not obliged to make utterances to please people to satisfy their itching ears. Many people hang around individuals operating in these realms in order to receive their wishful blessings. Although God will bless our wishes, we should be careful of our motives.

## Hunger and thirst for righteousness

The presence of the prophetic attracts hunger for righteousness and thirst for the Word of God.

## Itching ear or expression of anxiety

All ears are usually popped open and some ears begin to itch when the prophetic is noted.

# An Awakening

## Coveting of similar gifts or ability

Everyone feels like a child of God, and everyone has the desire to belong to God. Whenever we come across other people who have the ability to display prophetic or revelatory instinct, we are tuned to wake up and discover ourselves. In the process, we slip into a realm of realization and we start having flashbacks to where we first met the Lord. As we process our flashback memories, we sometimes slip into any of the following:

- Building of hope—I can also do it.

- Expression of envy—I can do it better (why not me?).

- Expression of regret—I should have responded to the initial opportunity offered me (the reality of our shortcomings and errors begin to dawn on us).

- Expression of self-pity—I wish I could get another chance (failure and self-disappointment may push us into depression).

# Chapter 2

# DIFFERENTIATING THE CALL FROM THE GIFT

**M**ORE OFTEN THAN not people are not able to differentiate between a call and a gift. People mistake a call for a gift; hence the gift of inspiration has been misunderstood as the office of the prophet.

I used to belong to a non-denominational fellowship in the late 1970s to early 1980s where the manifestation of prophecy and other revelatory gifts were highly adored and expected at every meeting. Every weekend, people traveled from far and near to participate in this fellowship because of the open acceptance of the demonstration of the gifts of prophecy and other revelatory gifts.

During the fellowship, the session for worship and

adoration, which normally preceded the praise and celebration session, was the core of the fellowship. It was a moment when God was expected to speak to His people. Every one was all ears and attentive to the spiritual realm. It was as though all had been carried from earth into the third heaven—no feelings of flesh, but heavenly feelings. With rapt attention to enter the Holy of Holies, worshipers positioned themselves in different prayer postures: some lying on the floor, some on bended knees, some sitting with their heads bowed, others kneeling down or standing with their hands raised, ready to receive from the throne of heaven.

There was intense attention as everyone opened up to receive and be used of the Lord. Both young and old, great and small, members and visitors were welcomed to demonstrate their revelatory gifts openly. There were no restrictions. It was Pentecost in action and the outpouring was great.

In the midst of worship, there would be a sudden outpouring of the presence of the Lord, during which individuals who had the revelatory gifts received from the Lord. At another level, there would suddenly be a drumming of tongues and groaning in the spirit. Some were crying, some laughing, some singing, some wailing, some screaming, some weeping, some sobbing, and some rolling on the floor while others stayed quiet observing, listening, writing, or taking in whatever was being said or done.

The majority of the participants were youth from high schools, colleges, and universities with very few from the working class. The prophetic word that poured out from heaven related to events that were to take place in all realms of government and nations around the world, and the revival that would sweep across the nation.

The prophetic word also emphasized the need for individuals to prepare themselves to take the gospel of our Lord Jesus Christ unto the nations. Government officials got wind of the prophecies and sent security personnel who came in to record the messages. Eventually most of the government officials that came into the meeting surrendered their lives to Christ Jesus; then similar fellowship meetings began to spring up across the nation, wherein charismatic churches were birthed and great miracles were witnessed as the Word of the Lord came to pass.

Today the majority of the young individuals that participated are in ministry fulfilling the call of God as it was revealed in that fellowship. I am one of the individuals that benefited from it. Through that fellowship my prophetic gifting and ability were developed with clarity.

However, there were different levels of prophetic manifestation that were demonstrated during the fellowship. There were people who could control themselves and the utterances that were made. There were people who had no self-control and would cry and scream before the prophetic could be released through their mouths. Some made so much noise that you could hardly hear or understand what they had to say. The manner of presenting the prophetic utterance revealed the difference between someone operating in the office of the prophet and a person exercising the gift of prophecy.

I noted that people who operated in the office of the prophet often handled the message with maturity to the understanding of all. People operating in the gift of prophecy would usually want to get into a state of ecstasy, want to speak very fast, and have little or no self-control. Such people want to demonstrate their gifts at all times, even when it is not convenient, and they are easily offended when they are not permitted to do so at will. Some of them also think that unless they speak in tongues, the prophetic word cannot come forth or it would not be real. These categories of people are quick to declare themselves as prophets because some of the utterances made eventually came to pass.

A person operating in the office of the prophet can carry a message to maturity like a pregnancy. The prophetic word operates with time and season. This chapter will discuss the difference between the gift of prophecy and the office of the prophet.

## A Gift

A gift is either a special capability or an endowment with which one is born. It is also a present that is given to a person, irrespective of who or what the person is. Giving out a present to somebody has nothing to do with the job or position that the person occupies. It is simply an endowment or talent that enables a person to display a unique aptitude or faculty in an endeavor. Such a unique capability may enhance a person's performance in a professional or occupational disposition.

The gift of the Spirit is a present that God bestows upon a person when one accepts Jesus Christ as Lord and Savior. God gives a believer gifts to enhance their relationship with Him, and also to strengthen their faith in Christ. The gifts of the Spirit encourage a believer to have a father-child relationship with the Lord.

The gift of prophecy is one of the nine gifts of the Spirit indicated in 1 Corinthians 12:8–10. This gift can manifest during a fellowship of the brethren and church services, especially during a session of praise and worship.

- A gift is an enhancer.

- A gift is a freewill offering.

- A gift does not require accountability.

- A gift does not require any form of obligation.

- A gift may be useful or useless to the recipient.

- A recipient may appreciate or acknowledge a gift.

- A gift may be a need or a want.

- A gift may not have value.

# A Call

A call is an office—a professional or occupational responsibility. It is an official duty where responsibilities are carried out and records are kept.

A call is administration oriented, while a gift is like a vapor in the air or wind. Although you may keep a record of a gift for evidential purpose, it is not an office. However, a gift can enhance a call in an office.

A call into the office of the prophetic is an occupation of one aspect of the five-fold ministries of Ephesians 4:11. It requires specific calling and anointing from God. The office of the prophet is a profession. It is a whole duty that occupies one's life. Therefore the prophet stays in the presence of God as a full-time duty to listen and hear directions.

The focus of the prophetic office is to stay in the presence of God for hours, days, and weeks, just as a secular professional individual stays on the job to fulfill his occupational task. Like a professional wakes up to go to his or her employment in the morning, a person fulfilling the office of a prophet wakes up and reports in the presence of God with his writing materials ready to receive instructions and directions. For instance, Moses, Daniel, Ezekiel, and Jeremiah were prophets who received divine instructions that required them to write as the Lord spoke. These prophets carried out their assignments with a high level of professionalism.

Moses was divinely prepared by God to occupy the office of a prophet by receiving all fundamental training that was needed to carry out his professional vocation of leading the people of Israel out of Egypt through the desert. As a prince in Egypt, Moses learned how to conduct himself in the royal palace before the king and also how to take and implement royal instructions from the seat of authority.

The royal training that Moses received enabled him to recognize and obey the authority of God. So Moses was able to take and follow a step-by-step instruction from the Almighty God to lead the children of Israel.

Moses's relationship with Jethro also taught him the lesson of the desert and the handling of a flock as a shepherd. The desert training enabled Moses to lead a multitude through the desert by following a day-to-day instruction from the Lord.

God prepared Moses to relate with Him, the King of Glory in the realm of royalty and also trained him to instruct the children of Israel in the realm of leadership to shepherd his flock through the desert to the Promised Land. Every challenge that Moses ever encountered was part of preparation to his call as a prophet of the Lord.

The office of the prophet is a perpetual calling. Even if God repents that He anointed the prophet, He still does not take away the office from a person until his or her call to glory—death—just like King Saul remained in office until his death.

But the gift of prophecy can fade away if it is not properly nurtured. However, God does not repent of giving one a gift even when it is misused. A gift is like a Christmas or birthday card. The giver does not regret giving it, even if it is even dumped into the garbage can at the end of the day.

- A call is a service that fulfills an office.
- A call is a profession: it gives hope for a living.
- A call is an occupation: it requires accountability.
- A call is an obligated responsibility: one is compelled to comply.
- A call is a lifetime endeavor that fulfills destiny.
- A call requires commitment, dedication, faithfulness, honesty, and loyalty.
- A call requires accountability and developmental abilities: a report is demanded.
- A call requires training and studiousness: qualification.

## The Prophetic Utterance

Just like the prophetic gift, the prophetic utterance demands a professional or mature presentation. A person operating in the prophetic office usually receives messages in advance, and has to pray for the time and season to deliver the message. Sometimes the messages are for instant delivery and sometimes they are not. The message or revelation may be in the form of word of wisdom, word of knowledge, discernment of spirits, or other channels. Unlike the gift of prophecy, the prophet has control over the dispensation and delivery of the message or revelation at hand.

## The Gift of Prophecy

The gift of prophecy is an inspirational utterance that is exercised by people who are not necessarily operating in the prophetic office. Every Christian may prophesy at one time or other to inspire, exhort, or encourage the body of Christ. The privilege of exercising the gift of prophecy on one or two occasions does not make a person a prophet.

Some people may flow in the gift of prophecy often or give prophecy every now and then; yet they are not prophets, for they are not able to speak freely or deliver the word without being in an atmosphere in which the gift will be received. Most people operating in the gift of prophecy usually need a vicarious and ecstatic state of emotion to exercise the gift. It is often impossible for people to exercise the gift of prophecy without being unconscious.

Although the gift of prophecy is not an office, it enhances a prophet's rhetoric ability in delivering God's message in a public setting. Some prophets are not oratorical; hence they stumble or stammer with their words and shy away from public speaking. Thus, other than dealing with individuals, they prefer not to speak in public. Such individual prophets usually need an ecstatic motivation such as the inspirational gift of prophecy to operate effectively in public.

Prophets who are shy often keep their eyes closed before operating in the euphoric realm. Prophets who are bold and aggressive will move with demonstrative actions while they deliver the Word of the Lord.

## A Talent

A talent is an inborn ability that is not learned but is naturally exhibited. A person who is naturally talented in an art is able to use it without receiving training, while others must be trained to do be able to exhibit the same art. A talent can be a vocation, which could be an occupation for producing an income and profit-making endeavor. Inborn talents that could become a vocation include: playing of musical instruments, singing, dancing, writing, cooking, sewing, etc.

## Not a Talent

The office of the prophet and the gift of prophecy are not talents. As mentioned earlier in this chapter, the office of the prophet is a call while the gift of prophecy is an inspirational present or gift to the body of Christ. Although there are people born with unique utterances that are either advisory or predictive, such ability is a talent that can be described as a gift, but not a gift of a word of wisdom or a gift of a word of knowledge—of the nine gifts of the Holy Spirit. There are people who display unique talents, yet they are not Christians and have no connection with the Holy Spirit.

When I was young in the ministry, I used to spend many hours in prayer seeking direction from the Lord. I would stay in the presence of the Lord for two to three hours every night. Once a month, I would spend a weekend in prayer camp. The more time I spent in the presence of the Lord, the lighter I felt in the spirit and the clearer the revelations I received.

Every night when I stayed in the presence of the Lord, my daily activities were revealed to me in a form of a movie. It was as though every activity that would happen in my environment was previewed to me in revelation. The revelatory preview included matters of governmental concerns, organizational decisions, church or ministry activities, and individual encounters and experiences. Sometimes it was as though a chain of activities were being repeated to me as they manifested in reality.

Before people came over to me for counseling, I would know ahead of time. Sometimes the Lord revealed their names, their problems, and solutions for which some individuals were coming to seek counsel. And I would be prepared to receive them.

Although the manifestation of the office of the prophet was with me from my early childhood, I did not know what it was until I went to high school. When I was in high school, my principal recognized this ability, and would usually call me into his office to ask me for advice on decisions he was making. He would relate an incident to me and then ask me to suggest a judgment. He would then caution me not to discuss the matter with any of the students or the teachers.

Persons with such unique utterances are known as wise men or wise women. They function well as counselors and advisors because their utterances are revealing and successful. However, they are not all prophets, but they can be trained to hold or operate in the office of the prophet. Some of these wise men and women who are not Christians usually practice the act of divination, spiritism, or magic (the obeah man, the warlock, the juju man, or the witch doctor).

## Difference Between a Man-made Gift and a Divine Gift

There are different types of gifts, and for the purpose of this study, it is important to explain the meaning of certain gifts and also distinguish between a man-made gift and a divine gift.

## Divine Gift

Persons called into prophetic office are usually endowed with divine gifts to enable them function effectively in the realm of their endeavors. Divine gifts are meant to enhance the prophet's abilities and performances. They are also meant to propel the prophet to achieve his or her destiny.

## God's gift makes the prophet

The Scripture states that the gift of a man makes room for him and brings him before great men (Prov. 18:16). The divine gift gives opportunity to the prophet to rise and shine among others.

## God's gift as a driver to destination

God's gift drives you to your destination. Through divine gifts, a prophet who may never have the opportunity to meet with kings and dine with princes by merit may be granted divine favor to relate with great men and women in authority.

## Propellant for fulfillment

When a divine gift is well managed, it becomes a propellant for a person called into the prophetic office to step into his or her destiny to experience fulfillment.

## Destiny oriented

Usually divine gifts are destiny oriented. As an enhancer, divine gifts enable a potential prophet to display unique abilities and near perfection performance.

## God tests with gifts

During our preparation to assume the position of a prophet, God takes us through various trials by putting certain gifts into our hands. Also, besides divine gifts, sometimes God releases other gifts to prepare us for a greater blessing. The manner in which we handle the initial gifts may determine our foundation and readiness to receive the empowerment to occupy the prophetic office. Therefore for us to occupy and fulfill the prophetic office:

- Our ability to handle treasure is tested.

- Our ability to keep records is tried.

- Our ability to give accountability is examined.

### God's gift builds up the prophet

*Power of utilization*

Divine gifts ignite the source of power that enables the prophet to utilize his or her ministry with confidence.

*Wisdom is built and developed*

The prophet builds up his ministry by applying wisdom and understanding to his utterances and presentations, irrespective of the messages received.

# Man-made Gift

When I was a journalist, I realized that giving out seasonal greeting cards and hand-outs during festivities like Christmas and New Year's is a big deal among corporate bodies and institutions. Media houses use the handouts sent to editors and field reporters as a yardstick to determine what kind of story should be published and which journalist should be placed on certain areas of assignment.

Journalists who usually received good handouts and

also shared their handouts or gratuities with their editors were easily promoted. Thus these journalists were often given respectable bylines as their stories were given prominent attention on prime pages.

Also, corporate institutions that gave media editors and journalists sponsorships and good adverts were given a place of importance in the media, even if their stories or materials were not strongly newsworthy. Some journalists lost their positions because they touched the sacred cows that fed the big bus in the media with special gifts. (The sacred cows are the business magnate and organizations that have constant advertisement slots in the media.) Although the stories were true, the poor journalists were made scapegoats because they did not know or understand the politics of handouts and man-made gifts.

Similarly, many people are hooked up to relationships they do not want to be in because their partners were introduced to them as a reward—man-made gift. Others are managing to endure or tolerate certain relationships because they cannot afford to lose the man-made gifts attached to them.

Man-made gifts are not destiny oriented because they do not come from God. Man-made gifts are usually false and destructive. Usually man-made gifts have hidden agendas and could be bait for the enemy to strike.

Man-made gifts:

- Attract attention
- Gain favor

- Create a sense of belonging
- Gain identification and recognition
- Expect an exchange which is paramount
- May be competitive driven
- May have a hidden agenda

# Chapter 3

# TYPES OF PROPHET

THERE ARE DIFFERENT types of prophets in the Bible. Each prophet is called differently and assigned with specific messages that identify their roles and personalities. Although the basic functions of the prophetic ministry may be principally the same, there are gifting and unique abilities that differ in performance and presentation.

## The Validation Syndrome

### The godfather's syndrome

The godfather's validation syndrome is the system whereby a local hero manages to gain a reputation from his or her past glory to build a kind of kingdom that makes everyone to depend on him or her directly or indirectly. That kingdom is used to protect the godfather's personal image even if his or her reputation turns sour.

The fear of man is gradually culminating into hero worship around great ministers and mega church owners instead of applying the God-fearing antidote. Our character, divine calling, and the works of our hands no longer speak for us. Instead of praying and seeking God for wisdom and direction, we rather accept people by basing our judgment on what the godfathers recommend and what group a person affiliates with. It is a great thing to have a godfather who can stand with you to encourage your vision. All the same, it is dangerous if our godfathers are fretting with our destiny.

**The old prophet syndrome**

Old prophets can either be a blessing or a deterrent to upcoming prophets, because some of them are easily intimidated and also do not welcome the new things that God intends to do in a nation or locality. Some old prophets do not believe anyone can do better; so believe that no one should be allowed to rise higher than their own past performances.

> And, behold, there came a man of God out of Judah by the word of the LORD unto Bethel: and Jeroboam stood by the altar to burn incense. And he cried against the altar in the word of the LORD, and said, O altar, altar, thus saith the LORD; Behold, a child

shall be born unto the house of David, Josiah by name; and upon thee shall he offer the priests of the high places that burn incense upon thee, and men's bones shall be burnt upon thee. And he gave a sign the same day, saying, This is the sign which the LORD hath spoken; Behold, the altar shall be rent, and the ashes that are upon it shall be poured out. And it came to pass, when king Jeroboam heard the saying of the man of God, which had cried against the altar in Bethel, that he put forth his hand from the altar, saying, Lay hold on him. And his hand, which he put forth against him, dried up, so that he could not pull it in again to him. The altar also was rent, and the ashes poured out from the altar, according to the sign which the man of God had given by the word of the LORD. And the king answered and said unto the man of God, Intreat now the face of the LORD thy God, and pray for me, that my hand may be restored me again. And the man of God besought the LORD, and the king's hand was restored him again, and became as it was before. And the king said unto the man of God, Come home with me, and refresh thyself, and I will give thee a reward. And the man of God said unto the king, If thou wilt give me half thine house, I will not go in with thee, neither will I eat bread nor drink water in this place: For so was it charged me by the word of the LORD, saying, Eat no bread, nor drink water, nor turn again by the same way that thou camest. So he went another way, and returned not by the way that he came to Bethel.

Now there dwelt an old prophet in Bethel; and his sons came and told him all the works that the man of God had done that day in Bethel: the words which he had spoken unto the king, them they told also to their father.

And their father said unto them, What way went he? For his sons had seen what way the man of God went, which came from Judah. And he said unto his sons, Saddle me the ass. So they saddled him the ass: and he rode thereon, And went after the man of God, and found him sitting under an oak: and he said unto him, Art thou the man of God that camest from Judah? And he said, I am. Then he said unto him, Come home with me, and eat bread.

And he said, I may not return with thee, nor go in with thee: neither will I eat bread nor drink water with thee in this place: For it was said to me by the word of the LORD, Thou shalt eat no bread nor drink water there, nor turn again to go by the way that thou camest. He said unto him, I am a prophet also as thou art; and an angel spake unto me by the word of the LORD, saying, Bring him back with thee into thine house, that he may eat bread and drink water. But he lied unto him. So he went back with him, and did eat bread in his house, and drank water. And it came to pass, as they sat at the table, that the word of the LORD came unto the prophet that brought him back: And he cried unto the man of God that came from Judah, saying, Thus saith the LORD, Forasmuch as thou hast disobeyed the mouth of the LORD, and hast not kept the commandment which the LORD thy God commanded thee, But camest back, and hast eaten bread and drunk water in the place, of the which the LORD did say to thee,

Eat no bread, and drink no water; thy carcass shall not come unto the sepulchre of thy fathers.

And it came to pass, after he had eaten bread, and after he had drunk, that he saddled for him the ass, to wit, for the prophet whom he had brought back. And when he was gone, a lion met him by the way, and slew him: and his carcass was cast in the way, and the ass stood by it, the lion also stood by the carcass. And, behold, men passed by, and saw the carcass cast in the way, and the lion standing by the carcass: and they came and told it in the city where the old prophet dwelt. And when the prophet that brought him back from the way heard thereof, he said, It is the man of God, who was disobedient unto the word of the LORD: therefore the LORD hath delivered him unto the lion, which hath torn him, and slain him, according to the word of the LORD, which he spake unto him.

And he spake to his sons, saying, Saddle me the ass. And they saddled him. And he went and found his carcass cast in the way, and the ass and the lion standing by the carcass: the lion had not eaten the carcass, nor torn the ass. And the prophet took up the carcass of the man of God, and laid it upon the ass, and brought it back: and the old prophet came to the city, to mourn and to bury him. And he laid his carcass in his own grave; and they mourned over him, saying, Alas, my brother! And it came to pass, after he had buried him, that he spake to his sons, saying, When I am dead, then bury me in the sepulchre wherein the man of God is buried; lay my bones beside his bones: For the saying which he cried by the word of the LORD against the altar in Bethel, and against all the houses of the high places which are in the cities of Samaria, shall surely come to pass. After this thing Jeroboam returned not from his evil way, but made again of the lowest of the people priests of the high places: whosoever would, he consecrated him, and he became one of the priests of the high places. And this thing became sin unto the house of Jeroboam, even to cut it off, and to destroy it from off the face of the earth.

—1 KINGS 13:1–34, KJV

Sometimes people who are ignorant easily feel intimidated when they meet with people whose performances are quite different from what they are used to. People who have been hailed as heroes in prophetic ministry within their localities are easily intimidated when a new prophet comes into town and performs excellently. Instead of the local heroic prophets taking a friendly seat to learn new methods, to update their knowledge, and to boost their ability, they often take a defensive position. Rather, these sets of individuals would begin to run down the work of God, as though they are the final authority to decide on the salvation of the people in their localities.

For instance, as an evangelist that operates in prophetic deliverance ministry, I do not go into any nation, city, or town unless the Lord sends me. I have no mission in any place if the Lord does not send me with a specific message to meet a specific need. This is important because I always need to be equipped and empowered to go; we war not against flesh and blood but against powers and principalities of darkness. It is dangerous to go to war unprepared or when you are not sent. (See Ephesians 6:12.)

Once the Lord tells me to go into a particular nation, I will start to pray and make connections as He instructs and directs. I have come to realize that although the Lord may appoint somebody to help; the individuals may not be willing to obey the voice of God. Indeed I have come to realize how the heart of a person can be desperately deceitful, because if the Lord's instruction does not please him or her, he or she will certainly pay a deaf ear to Him with the pretence of seeking confirmation.

Some time ago, the Lord instructed me to go into a certain nation in Asia. Miraculously, I came across several individuals from that country who served as ministers. Instead of praying to seek the will of God, they told me point blank that their nation did not need the deliverance ministry or any type of School of Deliverance. In other words, everyone residing in that nation is perfect; therefore no one has spiritual problems to need a kind of deliverance of ministration. Meanwhile, that territory is dominated by the Buddhists and Hindus and other Eastern religions. Some denominations share their worship centers with the Buddhist temple.

One day I returned to the Lord with all the excuses that the ministers from this particular nation had given. Then the Lord reminded me that I do not need any minister's invitation to do his work in a nation. As He has commanded me from the beginning, all I needed was His instruction to go as He sends me.

My first point of contact in a nation is to spend time in intercessory warfare to release the people from spiritual blindness and deception so that the bonds of captivity would be broken and the prison gates opened. This reminder gave me strength to go into that Asian country as I have been going to other nations without invitation. Eventually, when I told one of the ministers that I was coming into that nation to pray even if there is no room for School of Deliverance, the man suddenly got a revelation in which God spoke to him to host me.

Later on, I discovered the old prophet syndrome was operating in that nation. There was a great manipulation by an old prophet who easily puts out any prophet who visits the nation. This old prophet is easily intimidated. During one of my visits, I noticed how the man has succeeded in controlling a majority of the independent church leaders in that nation. It seems as though the Christians in that nation no longer wait on God for divine direction, but rather on this old prophet to decide who should be allowed to share a pulpit. Is the pulpit for a human kingdom or God's kingdom? Who decides what God intends to do with His people?

Although this man does not understand deliverance ministration, he goes to the pulpit to nullify all the deliverances that took place in our meetings. Ignorantly, he fights against the kingdom of God to promote himself instead of praising God for the deliverance of the people who have been delivered from demonic oppression and interferences.

The old prophet syndrome can be deadly because people are prevented from experiencing the joy of their salvation. Meanwhile this old prophet operates a church in a satanic stronghold where occult religious temples are established. Instead of pulling down satanic strongholds, he focuses his time in the pulpit on pulling down the ministry of other ministers that are meant to advance the kingdom of God.

The old prophet is yet to understand the truth about what the pulpit is meant for. The pulpit is not meant for war against fellow Christians and ministers of God, even if they are not perfect; the pulpit is meant to advance the kingdom of God while we war against interfering spirits to pull down satanic strongholds.

Some old prophets have appointed individuals whom they believe will not expose their weaknesses to function as prophets to the people. Anyone whom the old prophets do not validate would likely be rejected by the locality without seeking the will of God. Thus anyone the local prophet validates is hailed and celebrated; hence, false prophets have taken over the scene and the people are led astray because of the godfather's validation syndrome.

In recent times, the media has been full of adopted and self-proclaimed prophets who bribed their way to the top by paying homage to old and celebrity prophets. Many ignorant people are swayed by the hyping of prophetic utterances cooked up to excite the itching ears who mistake sugarcoated words for divine blessings. Hence, many do not know the differences that exist in the prophetic realms of performance.

The call and the purpose for which a prophet is appointed often determine the kind of messages that a prophet will be inclined to proclaim. Although theological studies categorize the biblical personalities that functioned in this office as minor and major prophets, this author has made a further study into the situations and circumstances that motivated their call and the performances thereof.

This chapter discusses various types of prophets by their call and purpose in office. Types of prophets include: the typical or natural prophet, the charismatic prophet, the accidental prophet, the adopted prophet, and the assumed prophet.

## The Typical or Natural Prophet

A typical prophet is one that is predestined to be a prophet. A natural prophet is sent to the earth with a mission to occupy and fulfill a specific errand as a prophet. Some of the biblical personalities that could be described as natural prophets include: Jesus Christ, John the Baptist, Moses, Samuel, and Jeremiah.

### Jesus Christ

Jesus Christ was called by virtue of His position as the second person of the Trinity. He was prophesied from the very beginning after the fall of man in Genesis 3. His birth was further announced by several prophets, including Isaiah and also by an angel in Luke 1:31–33.

## John the Baptist

An angel visited his father, Zachariah, to announce the birth of John the Baptist. Following the announcement, Elizabeth, the wife of Zachariah, also had divine encounters to confirm the purpose of the birth of John the Baptist.

## Jeremiah

Scripture declares in Jeremiah 1:5 that before the prophet was conceived, God had already made a plan and purpose to send him on an errand to the earth. Jeremiah was sent as a prophet with a specific message to a particular people.

## Moses

There might not have been a record of a prophetic declaration before the birth of Moses, yet Biblical records show that his birth triggered a mass killing of babies born to the Hebrew families in his days. The intention of the killing was to eliminate the potential savior who had been sent to deliver Israel from the house of bondage.

Miraculously, the potential savior was delivered into the very hand of the killer to be protected in the royal palace of Pharaoh. Moses lived to fulfill his calling as a prophet and savior who delivered Israel out of bondage.

## The Charismatic Prophet

The charismatic prophet is an aggressive person with a charismatic aptitude. He or she is called into office by virtue of his or her spontaneous response to the need of a people. A charismatic prophet has some leadership skills and virtues. He or she is purposefully driven to deliver and achieve set goals and targets.

The charismatic prophet is anointed and very bold. He or she is confident and courageous. The person is certain that he or she is speaking on behalf of God and does not usually use the term, "Thus says the Lord." For instance, Elijah was a charismatic prophet who confidently declares directly thus, "…except at my word" (1 Kings 17:1). In his dealings with the widow of Zarephath also, Elijah did not mention the name of the Lord until when he was making a declaration with reference to what the Lord has spoken in (v. 14).

Similarly, Elijah gave a command to Obadiah to go tell Ahab his master that Elijah was here. Elijah did not mention the name of the Lord until he needed to convince Obadiah, so he said: "As the Lord of hosts lives, before whom I stand, I will surely present myself to him today" (1 Kings 18:15).

Other charismatic prophets include the four major biblical prophets—Isaiah, Jeremiah, Ezekiel, and Daniel. Their virtues were:

- Purpose oriented
- Focus motivated

- Achievement oriented

- Given to dynamic demonstrations

- Result oriented

# THE FOUR MAJOR PROPHETS

## Prophet Isaiah

### His personality

Prophet Isaiah can be described as the Old Testament prototype of Apostle Paul of the New Testament. His prophetic language was persuasive and his style of presentation was poetic.

### His call

Isaiah's vision and prophetic call was similar to God's presence at Mount Sinai and also at the dedication of the tabernacle in Exodus 19:16, 40:34–35, and 1 Kings 8:10–11:

- The influence of the divine glory

- The shaking of the earth

- The smoke

Israel heard a great noise, but Isaiah heard the seraphim choir among the coming of the great and glorious King. "Holy, holy, holy, is the LORD of hosts; The whole earth is full of His glory!" (Isa. 6:3).

His generation was not prepared for the coming of the Lord. Isaiah made a confession of sin on behalf of his people (Isaiah 6:5).

## His mission

He was a court prophet who stood within the divine counsel of the Most High God to herald the coming of God's kingdom. He was given the mandate to prepare the holy remnant for the Lord's glorious establishment of His kingdom. Isaiah saw the new world.

## His message

Isaiah presented Yahweh as the Holy One of Israel. In his prophetic call, Isaiah received a vision as a guiding force. His ministry focused on Yahweh's holiness, His kingdom, and His judgment.

Isaiah was consumed by the message he proclaimed on God's holiness, establishment of His kingdom, and judgment on humanity.

- Salvation appears twenty-six times in the book of Isaiah.

- The book of Isaiah chapters 1–39 speak about man's great need for salvation.

- Chapters 40–66 speak about God's great provision for salvation.

# Prophet Jeremiah

## His call

Jeremiah was from a priestly lineage. He hailed from Anathoth in Benjamin, a Levitical city situated in the north of Jerusalem.

The Lord called Jeremiah to be His prophet and he remained faithful to the Lord. He was a prophet of national destruction and reconstruction. He was appointed over nations and kingdoms.

He was commissioned to uproot and tear down (Jer. 1:10–24). He announced the end of the Mosaic era and the beginning of a new era. He dialogued with the Lord and also interceded for God's people. He declared the end of God's patience and the appearance of judgment. He proclaimed God's wrath and condemnation. His Words ignited God's arrows of fire that consumes sin.

## His nature

He was severely tested, but he remained faithful to the Lord. He lived in constant tension between God's judgment in alienation and the promise of the new era of transformation.

He wanted to intercede for the people but his mission prohibited him. He was a prophetic intercessor. He wept over the message that he delivered to the people. God also reprimanded him for prophetic condemnation. God did not tolerate his harsh words and condemnation.

### His personality

Jeremiah was a heartbroken prophet with a heartbreaking message.

His message represented the burden on God's heart as Jesus was pierced in his side to bear our burden.

Jeremiah wept over the sin of the people as he presented a message of doom to a stiff-necked people.

He was a son of a priest, yet he was persecuted by priests and prophets.

Jeremiah was humiliated by the false prophet Hananiah.

Jeremiah was forbidden to marry and did not have any relationship because of the type of ministry that he was involved in.

### His message

Jeremiah's message was demonstrated by the functions of the potter:

- A ruined vessel can be repaired while still wet (Jer. 18:1–4); thus God delayed judgment and appealed for repentance.

- When the clay dries up, it is fit for the trash—condemnation (Jer. 19:10–11).

- When grace was over, refusal to repent led to Babylonian captivity, hence the cause for moral and spiritual catastrophe.

Jeremiah also preached on God's gracious hope and restoration. He spoke about the establishment of a new covenant (Jer. 31:33, Matt. 26:26–29).

# Prophet Daniel

### His personality

Daniel was a man with self-control.

He was a man of wisdom.

He applied the spirit of wisdom to his decision-making.

He maintained the fear of God in a pagan environment.

He was not perturbed by criticism and the challenges of accusation that surrounded the pagan environment where he was exiled.

He was devoted to Yahweh.

He was service oriented and diligent.

He exercised caution and discretion in all his endeavors.

He was content with the fear of God.

He did not seek power, rewards, or prestige for himself.

He demonstrated the fear of God before humans and the kings he served in foreign land.

### His call and exile

He was a teenage prophet in exile.

He was exiled along with prominent citizens, young men, and craftsmen from Jerusalem to Babylon.

He witnessed the devastation of Judah.

Daniel and his friends were selected to become the king's courtiers in a foreign land.

Daniel distinguished himself with a divinely endowed ability to interpret dreams.

Like Joseph in Egypt, Daniel was Yahweh's spokesman in a foreign court of Babylon.

Daniel served under three kings of Babylon for sixty-five years—Nebuchadnezzar, Belshazzar, and Darius from about 600–536 BC.

Daniel and his friends, Mishael, Hananiah, and Azariah, were placed in a pagan environment where they received pagan education for cultural integration.

The Babylonian education received at the Royal Academy enabled Daniel and his friends to acquire knowledge in history, structure, and cultural superiority to give them the aptitude for the king's administration.

The training was also designed to make Daniel and his friends to be without disability and be attractive in appearance.

The Babylonian education was also meant to equip Daniel and his friends to be well-informed, quick to understand, and qualified to serve in the king's court.

Ashpenaz was assigned to transform the Judean youths into cultured Babylonian princes, well-read in Babylonian language and literature, Aramaic, and other languages of the empire.

Daniel and his friends developed into competent and cultured statesmen.

They were expected to perpetuate the political, social, judicial, and economic structure of the Babylonian kingdom.

### His message

He proclaimed God's sovereignty over human affairs.

He insisted that the Most High God rules in the kingdoms of men and gives them to whomever He chooses (Dan. 4:25).

He declared that God directs the forces of history.

He demonstrated that God promises preservation and ultimate restoration.

Daniel contains over one hundred specific prophetic predictions that have manifested.

## Prophet Ezekiel

### His personality

He was born into a priestly family.

He was married and had a home.

He was a priest and a prophet.

He was trained in the law of the temple and to perform sacrifices.

He was also trained in international oriental education like Jeremiah.

He was skilled and knowledgeable in the world around him.

He was an artistic writer (Ezek. 1:3).

He was called to serve in the prophetic office at age thirty.

His father, Buzi, was a temple priest in Jerusalem.

Ezekiel was called into the prophetic ministry to be a prophet-watchman while in exile.

He had a vision of God's glory in exile like Moses in Exodus 33:18, 34:29–35 and Isaiah in Isaiah 6:1–5.

He was overcome by God's splendor because he received the glory in exile while Moses received it on Mount Sinai.

When Ezekiel saw the majestic glory of God, he fell down (slain in the spirit) in his human weakness, but the spirit of God raised him and empowered him (Ezek. 2:1–2).

The Spirit of God commanded him to minister to the exilic community (2:3–4).

**His message**

Ezekiel's concern was priestly emphasis on the temple, priesthood, sacrifices, and the Shekinah glory of God.

Ezekiel's message focused on the power and the plan of God.

As a priest, Ezekiel was responsible for teaching and

applying the message of guilt and condemnation through the Word and symbolic acts.

He preached the cause of captivity.

Like Jeremiah, he explained the purpose of judgment.

He exposed the lies of the false prophets who proclaimed peace when there was no peace.

He rebuked the use of magical charms to quell the plan of God to punish Israel's sins (their faith in magical charms on their wrists and the veils over their heads).

Like Isaiah and Jeremiah, he warned the people against the coming horror and hope.

Like Isaiah, he preached a message of consolation and restoration.

He spoke of God's return to His temple.

He saw the vision of His divine glory (chaps. 4–24).

He also spoke on the forthcoming judgment on Gentiles (chaps. 25–32).

He spoke about the restoration of Israel after the overthrow of Jerusalem (chaps. 33–48).

He spoke about the comfort and consolation of Israel with the illustration of the valley of dry bones (chap. 37).

### Ezekiel as a prophet-watchman

As a prophet-watchman in exile:

Ezekiel was an instrument of warfare (Ezek. 3:8–9).

He was a strength and protection for the people in exile (2:6–7).

He was a watchman over Israel (3:17–21).

He forewarned the people about what God intends to do.

He prepared the people for God's plans and purpose.

He explains the people's responsibilities towards the prophetic message.

He encouraged the people to repent.

He emphasized an individual's actions and responsibilities (9:8).

### Ezekiel as a suffering servant

Like Jeremiah, Ezekiel suffered for his people vicariously and empathetically.

He experienced the siege, deportation, and exile of Judah (3:22–5:17).

He was involved in the suffering of his people.

### Dramatic symbolism

Ezekiel lay on his side for 390 days.

He was bound with rope.

He ate defiled food (chap. 4).

He shaved off his hair with a sword and weighed it. He divided the shaved hair into three piles (Ezek. 5:1–4).

## The Accidental Prophet

The accidental prophets are a people who happen to be available in time of emergency or adversity when help is needed. Accidental prophets are not purposefully chosen, neither are they appointed because of credibility or integrity but are chosen in time of adversity. Accidental prophets may be divinely appointed, but they are neither part of the sons of the prophets nor from the priesthood family.

Accidental prophets only perform by saving a situation, and they are never there to continue with the mission. They may always appear at the spot when help is needed, but they cannot willingly flow in the office of a prophet on a regular basis. Accidental prophets are like angels on missions. Accidental prophets are often chosen by denominations or local churches to fill in the gap when there is a vacuum in the five-fold ministries.

- Not from the priestly or prophetic family
- Not by virtue of birth
- Called by virtue of discipline
- Called by virtue of educational and professional qualification
- By availability
- Divinely appointed

**Amos as an accidental prophet**

Amos was a shepherd and a farmer but was called into the prophetic office in a time of emergency. He only prophesied when the unction came upon him to do so. Amos described why and how God appointed him to stand in the gap and operate as a prophet in a state of emergency.

He said of himself:

*I was no prophet, Nor was I a son of a prophet,* But I was a sheepbreeder And a tender of sycamore fruit. Then the LORD took me as I followed the flock, *And the LORD said to me "Go, prophesy to My people Israel."*

—AMOS 7:14–15

Called:

- By virtue of knowledge of Scripture

- His lifestyle and discipline

- His professional distinction and excellence (7:14)

- His ability to understand the burden of the Lord (3:8; 7:15)

- Endowed with the Spirit of wisdom.

- A wise man.

## The Adopted and Hired Prophet

As the description goes, some people are adopted as prophet because they step into a situation in time of adversity, while some others are hired to occupy a position in the office of the prophet in order to meet spiritual needs. People are either adopted or hired to fulfill a prophetic role because the voice of a deity is needed for direction in time of trouble. Adopted and hired prophets are not natural or trained prophets but adopted by virtue of the help or assistance they offer in time of trouble.

In the Old Testament era, people who did not hail from a priestly or prophetic family were adopted as prophets by virtue of divine calling or an individual's discretion. There are many instances where individuals or groups of people adopted or hired gifted individuals to prophesy unto them.

In the New Testament era, persons called into prophetic office did not necessarily hail from a priestly or prophetic family. However, some folks posed as prophets because God once used them to meet a need at a crucial moment when they were available. Hence, such individuals were adopted or hired to give prophetic utterance.

In both the Old and New Testaments, there are instances that indicate that not all that prophesy are true prophets from the Most High God. In recent times, the church has been indulging in adopting and hiring individuals to sit in the office of the prophets in view of their prowess or performance. People are adopted or hired as prophets to fill in the gap because of situations and matters that arise. King Ahab adopted several prophets in his kingdom that prophesized lies to him.

> Also Jehoshaphat said to the king of Israel, "Please inquire for the Word of the LORD today." Then the king of Israel gathered the prophets together, about four hundred men, and said to them, "Shall I go against Ramoth Gilead to fight, or shall I refrain?" So they said, "Go up, for the Lord will deliver it into the hand of the king." And Jehoshaphat said, "*Is there not still a prophet of the LORD here, that*

*we may inquire of Him?*" So the king of Israel said to Jehoshaphat, "There is still one man, Micaiah the son of Imlal, by whom we may inquire of the LORD; but I hate him, because he does not prophesy good concerning me, but evil." And Jehoshaphat said, "Let not the king say such things!"

…Now Zedekiah the son of Chenaanah had made horns of iron for himself; and he said, "*Thus says the LORD; 'With these you shall gore the Syrians until they are destroyed.'*" And all the prophets prophesied so, saying, "Go up to Ramoth Gilead and prosper, for the LORD will deliver it into the king's hand." Then the messenger who had gone to call Micaiah spoke to him, saying, "Now listen, the words of the prophets with one accord encourage the king. Please, let your word be like the word of one of them, and speak encouragement."

And Micaiah said, "As the LORD lives, Whatever the LORD says to me, that I will speak." Then he came to the king; and the king said to him, "Micaiah, shall we go to war against Ramoth Gilead, or shall we refrain?" And he answered him, "Go and prosper, for the LORD will deliver it into the hand of the king!" So the king said to him, "How many times shall I make you swear that you tell me nothing but the truth in the name of the LORD?"

Then he said, "*I saw all Israel scattered on the mountains, as sheep that have no shepherd.* And the LORD said, 'These have no master. Let each return to his house in peace.'" And the king of Israel said to Jehoshaphat, "*Did I not tell you he would not prophesy good concerning me, but evil?*" … "The LORD has put a lying spirit in the mouth of all these prophets of yours, and the LORD has declared disaster against you."

...So the king of Israel and Jehoshaphat the king of Judah went up to Ramoth Gilead. ... *Now a certain man drew a bow at random, and struck the king of Israel between the joints of his armor.* So he said to the driver of his chariot, "Turn around and take me out of the battle, for I am wounded." ...*So the king died*, and was brought to Samaria. And they buried the king in Samaria.

—1 KINGS 22:5–8, 11–18, 23, 29, 34, 37,
EMPHASIS ADDED

The four hundred prophets in the king's court were appointed to encourage the king. Therefore, they prophesied lies to please and to win the king's favor.

The characteristic of adopted prophets are:

- Man-made prophets
- Deceptive utterances
- Human satisfaction
- Itching ears

### Gideon as an adopted prophet

Although God chose Gideon to lead Israel to war against their enemy, God did not make him a prophet or a ruler over His people. The people adopted him and things went wrong. He led them into idolatry and he was ensnared.

> And the men of Israel said to Gideon, "Rule over us, both you and your son, and your grandson also; for you have delivered us from the hand of Midian." And Gideon said to them, "I will not rule over you, nor shall my son rule over you; the LORD shall rule over you." Then Gideon said to them, "I would like to make a request of you, that each of you would give me the earrings from his plunder."... Then Gideon made it into an ephod and set it up in his city, Ophrah. *And all Israel played the harlot with it there. It became a snare to Gideon and his house.*
>
> —JUDGES 8:22–24, 27,
> EMPHASIS ADDED

### Micah and the hired prophet

Sometimes people who are called of God can wander into error because they do not stay in the place where God has called them to function. People who are too much of a hurry to be famous have often wandered out of God's timing and presence thinking that their personal decisions can help fulfill destiny. Micah was a young man who stole eleven shekels of silver from his mother. Although the mother had cursed the thief who stole the silver, the mother later reversed the curse into a blessing when Micah confessed that he took it. The following Scripture passage reveals how a Levite left his appointed place of service and wandered into Micah's idolatrous camp to serve as a hired priest and prophet to Micah and later the tribe of Dan.

> And there was a man of mount Ephraim, whose name was Micah. And he said unto his mother, The

eleven hundred shekels of silver that were taken from thee, about which thou cursedst, and spakest of also in mine ears, behold, the silver is with me; I took it. And his mother said, Blessed be thou of the Lord, my son. And when he had restored the eleven hundred shekels of silver to his mother, his mother said, I had wholly dedicated the silver unto the Lord from my hand for my son, to make a graven image and a molten image: now therefore I will restore it unto thee. Yet he restored the money unto his mother; and his mother took two hundred shekels of silver, and gave them to the founder, who made thereof a graven image and a molten image: and they were in the house of Micah. And the man Micah had an house of gods, and made an ephod, and teraphim, and consecrated one of his sons, who became his priest. In those days there was no king in Israel, but every man did that which was right in his own eyes.

And there was a young man out of Bethlehem-judah of the family of Judah, who was a Levite, and he sojourned there. And the man departed out of the city from Bethlehemjudah to sojourn where he could find a place: and he came to mount Ephraim to the house of Micah, as he journeyed. And Micah said unto him, Whence comest thou? And he said unto him, I am a Levite of Bethlehemjudah, and I go to sojourn where I may find a place. And Micah said unto him, Dwell with me, and be unto me a father and a priest, and I will give thee ten shekels of silver by the year, and a suit of apparel, and thy victuals. So the Levite went in. And the Levite was content to dwell with the man; and the young man was unto him as one of his sons. And Micah consecrated the Levite; and the young man became his priest, and was in the house of Micah. Then said Micah, Now know I that the LORD will do me good, seeing I have a Levite to my priest.

—JUDGES 17:1–13, KJV

Just before the Lord released me to start traveling to the nations, He gave me some warning statements that I needed to guard me against practices that would ensnare my ministry and relationship with Him the Lord. One of the instructions the Lord gave me was to avoid being a personal prophet to individuals and their friends or family; otherwise they would buy my spirit with money and gifts, and I would be tempted to please them in all things. I would also find myself prophesying sweet lies instead of stating the exact truth that may include rebuke, correction, and edification.

Each time I come across people who would want to use my spirit for selfish benefit, the Lord reminds me that my spirit and anointing is not for sale, but for service unto the Lord. In view of the fact that I will not succumb to being used to fulfill selfish gains, many individuals have not been very happy with me. I will always tell the truth no matter what. God called me, and I will give account of my service to the Lord at the end of the day. The prophetic ministry is very attractive but delicate. It can easily be adulterated for hiring. Many true prophets have suddenly been hired for financial gain because they have either lost their divine positioning or wandered away from their divine destination.

This passage reveals a realm of deception that is currently sweeping across local denominations. Some of the celebrity church founders in our localities are symbols of Micah who once stole his mother's wealth, created a god for himself, and appointed one of his sons as a priest. Eventually, Micah laid hold of a Levite, who was supposed to be a man of God from Bethlehem-Judah, consecrated him, and then hired him to be his priest.

The following passage also reveals how the adulteration of our church pulpits has become a vogue of attraction for innocent people who are seeking divine help to fulfill their destiny. Without considering the status of the corrupted Levite priest, the family of Dan was swayed by a deceptive miracle and snatched the false prophet from Micah's temple.

> In those days there was no king in Israel: and in those days the tribe of the Danites sought them an inheritance to dwell in; for unto that day all their inheritance had not fallen unto them among the tribes of Israel. And the children of Dan sent of their family five men from their coasts, men of valour, from Zorah, and from Eshtaol, to spy out the land, and to search it; and they said unto them, Go, search the land: who when they came to mount Ephraim, to the house of Micah, they lodged there. When they were by the house of Micah, *they knew the voice of the young man the Levite*: and they

turned in thither, and said unto him, *Who brought thee hither? and what makest thou in this place? and what hast thou here?* And he said unto them, Thus and thus dealeth Micah with me, and *hath hired me, and I am his priest.* And they said unto him, *Ask counsel, we pray thee, of God, that we may know whether our way which we go shall be prosperous.* And the priest said unto them, Go in peace: before the LORD is your way wherein ye go.

Then the five men departed, and came to Laish, and saw the people that were therein, how they dwelt careless, after the manner of the Zidonians, quiet and secure; and there was no magistrate in the land, that might put them to shame in any thing; and they were far from the Zidonians, and had no business with any man. And they came unto their brethren to Zorah and Eshtaol: and their brethren said unto them, What say ye? And they said, Arise, that we may go up against them: for we have seen the land, and, behold, it is very good: and are ye still? be not slothful to go, and to enter to possess the land. When ye go, ye shall come unto a people secure, and to a large land: for God hath given it into your hands; a place where there is no want of any thing that is in the earth. And there went from thence of the family of the Danites, out of Zorah and out of Eshtaol, six hundred men appointed with weapons of war. And they went up, and pitched in Kirjathjearim, in Judah: wherefore they called that place Mahanehdan unto this day: behold, it is behind Kirjathjearim. *And they passed thence unto mount Ephraim, and came unto the house of Micah.*

*Then answered the five men that went to spy out the country of Laish, and said unto their brethren, Do ye know that there is in these houses an ephod, and teraphim, and a graven image, and a molten image?* now therefore consider what ye have to do. *And they turned thitherward, and came to the house of the young man the Levite, even unto the house of Micah, and saluted him.* And the six hundred men appointed with their weapons of war, which were of the children of Dan, stood by the entering of the gate. And *the five men that went to spy out the land went up,* and *came in thither, and took the graven image, and the ephod, and the teraphim, and the molten image: and the priest stood in the entering of the gate with the six hundred men that were appointed with weapons of war.* And these went into Micah's house, and fetched the carved image, the ephod, and the teraphim, and the molten image. *Then said the priest unto them, What do ye? And they said unto him, Hold thy peace, lay thine hand upon thy mouth, and go with us, and be to us a father and a priest: is it better for thee to be a priest unto the house of one man, or that thou be a priest unto a tribe and a family in Israel? And the priest's heart was glad, and he took the ephod, and the teraphim, and the graven image, and went in the midst of the people.* So they turned and departed, and put the little ones and the cattle and the carriage before them. And when they were a good way from the house of Micah, the men that were in the houses near to Micah's house were gathered together, and overtook the children of Dan. And they cried unto the children of Dan. And *they turned their faces, and said unto Micah, What aileth thee, that thou comest with such a company? And he said, Ye have taken away my gods which I made, and the priest, and ye are gone away: and what have I more? and what is this that ye say unto me, What aileth thee?* And the children of Dan said unto him, Let not thy voice be heard among us, lest angry fellows run upon thee, and thou lose thy life, with the lives of thy household. And the children of Dan went their way: and when Micah saw that they were too strong for him, he turned and went back unto his house.

And they took the things which Micah had made, and the priest which he had, and came unto Laish, unto a people that were at quiet and secure: and they smote them with the edge of the sword, and burnt the city with fire. And there was no deliverer, because it was far from Zidon, and they had no business with any man; and it was in the valley that lieth by Bethrehob. And they built a city, and dwelt therein. And they called the name of the city Dan, after the name of Dan their father, who was born unto Israel: howbeit the name of the city was Laish at the first. *And the children of Dan set up the graven image: and Jonathan, the son of Gershom, the son of Manasseh, he and his sons were priests to the tribe of Dan until the day of the captivity of the land. And they set them up Micah's graven image, which he made, all the time that the house of God was in Shiloh.*

—JUDGES 18:1–31, KJV,
EMPHASIS ADDED

From the account of this passage, it is clear that when sin enters a camp and it is not dealt with diligently, there will be proliferation of corruption in the pulpit and men of God will be hired by individuals to fulfill the role of personal prophets and priests. The Levite wandered away from his divine positioning and became a priest on high demand among people who needed the blessings of the Most High God, but were not ready to dwell with truth and righteousness.

It is easy for a disobedient prophet to be on high demand, because they avail themselves for trade and not for divine usage. A priest or prophet who wants to please the world instead of God will eventually become a false prophet because he or she will usually concentrate on telling the people the glittering side of the story and avoid the preparatory and surgical part, which may reflect the challenges and difficulties that come with the package.

## The Assumed Prophet

Sometimes accidental and adopted prophets become assumed prophets because they were once used to meet a need or fulfill a mission. There are people who go about parading themselves as prophets because an utterance they made once came to pass. Assumed prophets behave like false prophets because they impose themselves upon people. They listen to gossips to formulate prophetic messages. They manipulate events and situations to create prophetic instances.

Assumed prophets make effort to enforce the

fulfillment of their utterances. Once upon a time, Saul prophesied and people were surprised and asked, "Is Saul also among the prophets?" (1 Sam. 10:11). Hence, Saul assumed that having once exercised the gift of prophecy which was meant to be a manifestation of his call into the kingly office, then he should also be qualified to offer sacrifices as expected of Samuel the prophet.

> So Saul said, *"Bring a burnt offering and peace offerings here to me." And he offered the burnt offering."*...And Samuel said, "What have you done?" Saul said, "When I saw that the people were scattered from me, and that you did not come within the days appointed, and that the Philistines gathered together as Michmash, then I said, 'the Philistines will now come down on me at Gilgal, and I have not made supplication to the LORD.' *Therefore I felt compelled, and offered a burnt offering."*
>
> And Samuel said to Saul, "You have done foolishly. You have not kept the commandment of the LORD your God, which He commanded you. For now the LORD would have established your kingdom over Israel forever. But now your kingdom shall not continue. The LORD has sought for Himself a man after His own heart, and the LORD has commanded him to be commander over His people, because you have not kept what the LORD commanded you."
>
> —1 SAMUEL 13:9, 11–14

As a result of his assumption, Saul encountered the wrath of God.

Characteristics of assumed prophets include:

- Self-appointed

- Self-imposing

- Manipulative

- Controlling

- Lying

- Deceptive

Deuteronomy 18:20–22 says:

> But the prophet who presumes to speak a word in
> My name, which I have not commanded him to
> speak, or who speaks in the name of other gods,
> that prophet shall die. And if you say in your heart,
> 'How shall we know the word which the Lord has
> not spoken?'—when a prophet speaks in the name
> of the LORD, if the thing does not happen or come
> to pass, that is the thing which the LORD has not
> spoken; the prophet has spoken it presumptuously
> you shall not be afraid of him.

# Chapter 4

# QUALITIES OF A PROPHET

THE PERSONALITY OF an individual who professes to be a prophet has often been used as a yardstick to determine the quality of the message that a prophet has to deliver. In view of that, the character of a person who gives prophetic utterances has been used as the basis for judging the prophetic word in many societies. This is because it is commonly believed that God is holy, therefore He will not make use of an unclean vessel.

The irony of the prophetic is that it is very revealing. Even non-churchgoers have a stereotyped idea of who a prophet should or should not be. The common question then is, if uncleanness is considered evil (as the characteristic of Satan), why would God use an unclean thing to fulfill a holy purpose? Several of these kinds of questions are asked before a prophetic word is received by some individuals, especially when the prophets concerned have questionable personalities.

In one of the fellowships that I used to be associated with, there was a young lady who used to exercise the gift of prophecy at every meeting. Once we closed our eyes for prayer, the lady would begin to prophesy. In fact, she claimed she was a prophetess and people referred to her as one. Meanwhile, her lifestyle was questionable because she had no control over her physical body and emotions.

One day she got angry and stormed out of a prayer meeting because she was asked to hold on until the appropriate time to release whatever message she had. Then moderator went on to say that the spirit of the prophet must be subject to the prophet.

This lady got angry and stormed out as she made ungodly comments like, "If you are true children of God, you would listen to the voice of God." She also stated that we were sinners and did not want to take her corrections and directives.

At the end of the fellowship meeting, a delegate was sent to her house to reconcile her behavior and also initiate peace with her. As a result of this visit, she was caught in an act of fornication with a married man who lived next door. It was a red-handed arrest in the sense that the party that visited her was ushered into her living room by her junior sister who was naïve. The bedroom door was left ajar while the party witnessed the scene of action openly.

Once again, she was outraged that the party had deliberately set her up to mess up her ministry and reputation. She even tried to make an accusation that the act was an attack from one of the men who had come to visit her. Unfortunately for her, there was a lady in the party. Otherwise the claim would have become a disgrace to the men, who initially did not want a female to be a part of the delegation.

The negative fruits that were gathered around the prophetess's life finally revealed who she was and her intentions to manipulate the fellowship meetings to satisfy her selfish ambition. Her claim of being a prophetess was exposed within a short period of time. It became very clear to everyone in the fellowship that if a message comes from the Lord, the vessel carrying the message must be able to exercise patience and wait for the appropriate time and season to deliver the message. Indeed, the spirit of the prophet is subject to the prophet. If God has spoken, allow God Himself to perform it.

Patience is one of the fruits of the spirit, while anger is one of the works of the flesh. Self-control is also one of the fruits of the spirit. A sincere prophet must have self-control over his or her character and public behavior. A sincere prophet must demonstrate a high quality of morality and distinguish himself or herself from others.

Based on the knowledge of my experience and ministerial activities, I usually advise young people not to put a demand on themselves by addressing themselves as prophets or prophetesses. Whenever you allow yourself to be called a prophet or prophetess, you place a high demand on your personality, public behavior, and reputation. If you are not able to maintain a high level of self-control, you will mess up your life and ministry. People often get offended when they are asked to keep it cool until they are matured enough to handle themselves and the demands that follow.

In another event, a lady that I would describe as Mollet was double-tongued and mischievous in her behavior. She was quarrelsome and ever ready to put up a fight, even during Sunday morning worship service. The ushers avoided her because she often challenged them.

One day Mollet gave an open prophecy during Sunday morning worship service, as she screamed at the top of her voice; and the word came to pass. Instantly, members of the church forgot about Mollet's notorious and disrespectful behavior and started to consult Mollet for prophecy. The pastor also referred to Mollet as prophetess. Church members began to visit Mollet's home for consultation. In view of that, she and her husband started a church based on her prophecies. Since she realized that her husband depended on her prophecies to make decisions, she also began to use prophecy to control their home and relationship. Every decision that was ever made was based on "thus saith the Lord."

At another time, Mollet prophesied that God was going to give them a house and a car at a certain date, so they would need to pack up their belongings and to go wait at a particular place to which the Lord would send the angel to deliver the car and the keys to their new home. Indeed there was a new apartment building that had just been completed so the husband had high hopes that God had indeed spoken. When they got to the spot and off-loaded their luggage by the car park, the building attendant approached them and told them that there were not any vacancies; but they insisted that the Holy Spirit had directed them. For weeks Mollet and her husband hung around the neighborhood but the "god" who gave them the promise never showed up. Everyday, people gathered around them to listen to prophecies. Eventually they ended up in the homeless people shelter.

Finally, Mollet's husband owned up to the fact that Mollet was a chronic liar who had indulged in con-artistry and spiritism in the past before they started going to church. Both of them had been consulting spiritism to influence their involvement in luring people to give them whatever they demanded. The incident of the prophecy that came to pass in the church service was not from God but from their spiritism. Since both the pastor and the church members believed in their utterances, they were hyped by those who consulted them.

Hence, the act increased to the point of conning a whole church with their prophetic manipulations. Mollet's husband was bitter because he felt the pastor should have discerned the spirit behind the prophecy and also should have cautioned them. Instead, the pastor referred to Mollet as a prophetess, so the whole church started to call Mollet prophetess. She was hyped by the people to prophesy lies and deception.

Once a self-proclaimed prophet gets upset, it is obvious that he or she is treading on a dangerous path, because anger is a sign of pride. When a person repels correction, it is a sign of an unteachable spirit. God always prunes his prophets and takes them through the refiner's fire which includes correction and pruning.

A prophet or prophetess who indulges in sin makes his or her body available for satanic usage. Does he or she at the same time expect the Lord Most Holy to also serve his children from the same dirty vessel? No, a vessel is either clean or dirty. God will not drink from an unholy vessel and will not use an unclean vessel to serve his children. It is unhealthy and dangerous.

Hence, it is very crucial that this chapter discuss the qualities of a prophet in order to understand the forum for both the personality and the quality of the message received.

## The Personality of a Prophet

Everyone has a concept of what a prophet should be—God's spokesman. Like Moses, he or she is expected to stay close to God and experience His presence. Therefore, he or she must be a person of excellence. Like Daniel, he or she must know all things and have an excellent spirit and high IQ. His or her personality and perception of things must be holy and pure.

Irrespective of what the human perception may be, a person representing God must be a man or woman of excellence. The person must be able to put up a unique standard in appearance and presentation. A prophet must not appear shabby and unkempt just because he or she has been on a long fast or has been in the presence of God for days.

A prophet is an ambassador of heaven. A prophet is a type of leader who directs the destiny of people. The prophet must therefore be on top and not below, above and not beneath. The prophet must be a man or woman of example, regardless of his or her academic endowment.

## The Background of a Prophet

The background of a prophet is very important in relation to certain messages that he or she often carries or presents. The Scripture has often revealed the background of a prophet in order to show the importance and relevance of the errand that a particular prophet is called to fulfill.

### Education and exposure

Academic education and professional training was relevant to the biblical prophets. An institution of prophetic training was in existence even in the days of Samuel and Elisha. The purpose of a prophetic academy or institution is to ensure that people called to fulfill the prophetic ministry are identified with a high sense of quality and excellence.

The Bible indicates that all of the major prophets

received some form of ministerial training. Among those listed to have been educated either as a priest or prophet were Ezekiel and Jeremiah.

### Persistency and consistency

A prophet must be persistent and consistent in the delivery and presentation of messages assigned to him. A prophet must not allow personal matters and environmental situations to interfere with either the message received or its delivery. The prophet must endeavor to act as a professional entity to fulfill an office. Thus he or she must be tenacious, steadfast, and un-moveable in the course of action. The fear of God must be invited to guard every step and action taken while fulfilling this office.

### Accuracy

The prophet must realize that he or she is a messenger. A messenger does not seek his or her own in the course of delivering an errand for the master but seeks to satisfy the master's goal. A messenger does not share in the glory of God but must endeavor to give all glory to God. Therefore the message must be delivered undiluted—as it is.

Except where it is necessary, a prophet must first deliver the whole message before making an attempt to interpret it. A prophet must not try to mix up the main message with an assumed meaning. Interpretation is not the same as the original message received. Therefore the message must be accurately presented before a meaning is added to it. A prophet must distinguish between the main message and the interpretation, so that the recipient will know where to draw the line between, "Thus says the Lord" and "Thus says my interpretation."

Once upon a time, I used to permit everyone to present whatever revelation they received during our prayer sessions. When I called for revelation, some people would start to interpret the revelation without telling us what the revelation was. On many occasions I interrupted them and asked what exactly they saw or heard. Some of them would be reluctant to say exactly what the revelation was but try to impose the interpretation on us. When they would finally stated exactly what they saw or heard, the actual revelation had no bearing on the interpretation they had given.

At a particular instance, a lady I will refer to as Pobsky saw a vision in which another lady, Ramaha, was feeding babies. Pobsky assumed that Ramaha was seeking pregnancy to have babies so she started giving interpretation that Ramaha would be pregnant in the next few weeks and give birth at a particular time of the season. I immediately felt in my spirit that the interpretation was wrong, so I interrupted Pobsky and asked her, "What exactly did you see or hear?" She then narrated exactly what she saw after I had insisted that what we needed was exactly what she saw, not the interpretation of what she assumed.

I then turned to Ramaha and asked, "Are you seeking pregnancy for babies?" Ramaha said, "No, I already have eight adult children and I am a grandmother of six." At this point, I turned to Ramaha who was then visiting our fellowship for the first time and said, "I feel you are thinking of setting up a day care center that would accommodate both your grandchildren and others." She said, "Exactly—I came in here for prayer with regards to that." Then she opened her bag and showed us a document for her registration.

Instead of Pobsky accepting her mistake and apologizing, she started claiming that she was a prophetess and that she heard the Lord giving the interpretation. In any case, it was too late for the grandmother of six to seek any pregnancy.

There is nothing wrong with interpreting a divine revelation if the Lord authorizes you to do so. But be careful not to inject your personal understanding into the original message.

Many prophets have been tagged false because they did not distinguish between the original message and the interpretation added to the message. Whenever the original message is attached to interpretation, there is bound to be an error and misinformation. Therefore the original word must be separated from the assumed meaning. Otherwise the truth of the matter will be hidden from the understanding of the whole message. Consequently, the purpose and impact will be swallowed up by assumption and false excitement.

**Unique distinctions**

Every prophet has a unique ministry and message for which he is identified from Biblical times. Like King

David, a prophet may be poetic in his manner of presentation; or like Ezekiel, a prophet may be demonstrative or artistic. Each person must identify their unique abilities and not try to be like somebody else while performing their prophetic functions. Copying other people's styles may affect the meaning and impact of the message.

## Poetic prophet

A poetic prophet is one that is blessed with the art of speaking rhythmically as though one is singing. Some poetic prophets sing their words while some speak as though they are reciting an already written poem.

Similarly, there are prophets who write out their messages in poetic verses, while they express themselves by speaking in the same manner. King David and Isaiah were poetic prophets.

## Artistic prophet

The artistic prophet receives and delivers messages by using descriptive or illustrative terms. Some of the terms used are demonstrative descriptions of images. That means the prophet receives his messages in a form of audio-visuals and as such makes a presentation in the same manner. Some prophets see pictures of actions of things that have happened and things yet to come as though they were physically present at the scene. Therefore they become artistically demonstrative in their presentations. Jeremiah and Ezekiel were artistic prophets.

## Demonstrative prophet

Demonstrative prophets usually use live illustrations to present their messages. Some charismatic prophets are demonstrative. John the Baptist was a demonstrative prophet. He spoke and acted the prophecy about the baptism of the Lord Jesus Christ instantly.

## Dramatic prophet

Hosea was a dramatic prophet. He acted out his messages with his marriage to a harlot, Gomer. He also bore children with Gomer to further demonstrate the relationship between the Almighty God (Yahweh) and Israel, who was living a promiscuous life.

## Persuasive prophet

A persuasive prophet is one whose role spans beyond receiving messages from God to also being involved in the affairs of the state. That means a prophet may be called to perform the double role of receiving and delivering the oracle of God. A persuasive prophet's utterances can influence governmental decisions.

Moses and Samuel were both persuasive prophets. Moses instituted the law and ordinances and also installed the leadership of Israel. Samuel was a prophet and a judge. He was also involved in the installation of the early kings of Israel.

Irrespective of the unique ability that a prophet may possess, there are common factors that are predominant in the prophetic ministry. These factors reveal the author of the message as the Almighty God and the vessel of delivery as a human being. If indeed the message comes from God, then humans cannot motivate the manifestation and the fulfillment. Therefore a true prophet of God must be consciously aware of the following.

A Prophet of God

- Does not impose

- Does not go unless sent

- Identifies the message

- Understands the role to be performed

- Analyzes the message for the appropriate season

- Fears the Lord

- Consciously walks and works in obedience

- Lives a sober and humble life

- Listens and follows instructions and directions

# Chapter 5

# FUNCTIONS OF THE PROPHETIC MINISTRY

THE DEFINITION OF a prophet is not too far from the functions performed in the office of the prophet. The prophet is known by the role he plays in the lives of the people he is sent or assigned to. This chapter will discuss the regular and combined functions of the prophet in the life of a nation, a church, an organization, a family, an individual, and generally.

## The Regular Office

The regular office of the prophet includes foretelling the Word of the Lord, teaching and guiding, counseling, interceding, and judging, among other activities.

Some of the general functions performed in the prophetic office are built on the foundation outline found in Deuteronomy 18:15–22 (KJV):

> The LORD thy God will raise up unto thee a Prophet from the midst of thee, of thy brethren, like unto me; unto him ye shall hearken; According to all that thou desiredst of the LORD thy God in Horeb in the day of the assembly, saying, Let me not hear again the voice of the LORD my God, neither let me see this great fire any more, that I die not. And the LORD said unto me, They have well *spoken that* which they have spoken. *I will raise them up a Prophet from among their brethren, like unto thee, and will put my words in his mouth; and he shall speak unto them all that I shall command him.* And it shall come to pass, that whosoever will not hearken unto my words which he shall speak in my name, I will require it of him. But the prophet, which shall presume to speak a word in my name, which I have not commanded him to speak, or that shall speak in the name of other gods, even that prophet shall die. And if thou say in thine heart, How shall we know the word which the LORD hath not spoken? When a prophet speaketh in the name of the LORD, if the thing follow not, nor come to pass, that *is* the thing which the LORD hath not

spoken, *but* the prophet hath spoken it presumptuously: thou shalt not be afraid of him.

—EMPHASIS ADDED

Evidently, a true prophet is answerable to God. Therefore such a person must spend time in His presence for divine instructions and directions in order to present a pure word from the heart of God to the people. Below are some of the functions that a person fulfilling the office of a prophet must perform.

**To hear the voice of God**

What distinguishes a prophet from other ministers in the five-fold ministry is the fact that he or she has a unique audience with God. The prophet is known for his regular visits into the presence of God, which enables him or her to listen and hear the voice of God. The prophet represents the Lord as an ambassador and a spokesperson. The prophet is an accredited diplomat for God and heaven.

For instance, Aaron was a priest, yet he did not have regular access into the presence of God. Aaron had the opportunity to go with Moses only when he was invited. Aaron had access into the inner court of the tabernacle and the holy of holies, but did not have regular access into the unique presence to have conversations with the Almighty God as Moses did. Aaron could go into the holy of holies only at specified times of the season when the law permitted him to do so. Although we are no longer under the law, the rule still stands directly and indirectly.

**To provide a link between God and man**

As a divine diplomat, the prophet is called to provide a link between God and the people. The link that the prophet provides makes him or her an intercessor that carries the voice of mankind and the voice of the Almighty God. Often people depend on the prophet to contact God on their behalf. Because of unconfessed sin and unforgiveness, not everyone has access into the presence of the Lord.

In recent times, people visit the office of a prophet or attend conferences in order to seek consultative attention through a prophet. The practice of seeking prophetic consultation was a norm in the biblical days. It has now become rampant as people desire to know the will of God and the path that leads to their divine destiny.

**To present the message of the Lord to the people**

It is the duty of the prophet to present the Word of the Lord to the people undiluted, that is—"as it is." But the word must be declared in season—at the right time. Thus a prophet must listen and also be sensitive to respond to divine intuition to move and act in season and on time.

**To act as God's spokesperson**

The prophet must always remember that he or she is on an ambassadorial errand. Therefore a prophet must seek the will of the Master and not self-glory. He or she must present the Word of the Lord with honor and integrity.

## To intercede for the people

The prophet must always seek to intercede for the people. Even if God is not pleased with the people, it is the duty of the prophet to stand in the gap and pray for divine intervention. The prophet must not encourage judgment and condemnation, but rather repentance and forgiveness.

For instance, when the children of Israel complained about food because they were not pleased with the manna, Moses went to God on behalf of the people. In his supplication, Moses laid down his life as a sacrifice to gain God's attention as he made a demand that gave God an option to either solve the problem or kill him—Moses.

And *when the people complained, it displeased the* LORD: *and the* LORD *heard it; and his anger was kindled; and the fire of the* LORD *burnt among them, and consumed them that were in the uttermost parts of the camp.* And the people cried unto Moses; and when Moses prayed unto the LORD, the fire was quenched. And he called the name of the place Taberah: because the fire of the LORD burnt among them.

And the mixt multitude that was among them fell a lusting: and the children of Israel also wept again, and said, Who shall give us flesh to eat? We remember the fish, which we did eat in Egypt freely; the cucumbers, and the melons, and the leeks, and the onions, and the garlick: But now our soul is dried away: there is nothing at all, beside this manna, before our eyes. And the manna was as coriander seed, and the colour thereof as the colour of bdellium. And the people went about, and gathered it, and ground it in mills, or beat it in a mortar, and baked it in pans, and made cakes of it: and the taste of it was as the taste of fresh oil. And when the dew fell upon the camp in the night, the manna fell upon it. Then Moses heard the people weep throughout their families, every man in the door of his tent: *and the anger of the LORD was kindled greatly; Moses also was displeased. And Moses said unto the LORD, Wherefore hast thou afflicted thy servant? and wherefore have I not found favour in thy sight, that thou layest the burden of all this people upon me? Have I conceived all this people? have I begotten them, that thou shouldest say unto me, Carry them in thy bosom, as a nursing father beareth the sucking child, unto the land which thou swarest unto their fathers? Whence should I have flesh to give unto all this people? for they weep unto me, saying, Give us flesh, that we may eat. I am not able to bear all this people alone, because it is too heavy for me._And if* thou deal thus with me, kill me, I pray thee, out of hand, if I have found favour in thy sight; and let me not see my wretchedness.

—NUMBERS 11:1–15, KJV,
EMPHASIS ADDED

The Lord expects a prophet to cry on behalf of the people and make intercession and supplication for them. A prophet does not encourage God to condemn or destroy the people as Jonah expected.

I have heard some "men of God" invoke curses on people and also utter words of destruction on members of their congregations. No matter the gravity of the sin committed, it is not proper for anyone to curse church members.

On another occasion, when the children of Israel provoked Moses over the issue of water, Moses was tempted to strike the rock instead of speaking to the rock, and that action affected his relationship with God. Hence, Moses did not see the promise land.

> Then came the children of Israel, even the whole congregation, into the desert of Zin in the first month: and the people abode in Kadesh; and Miriam died there, and was buried there. And *there was no water for the congregation: and they gathered themselves together against Moses and against Aaron.* And the people chode with Moses, *and spake, saying, Would God that we had died when our brethren died before the* Lord! *And why have ye brought up the congregation of the* Lord *into this wilderness, that we and our cattle should die there?* And wherefore have ye made us to come up out of Egypt, to bring us in unto this evil place? it is no place of seed, or of figs, or of vines, or of pomegranates; neither is there any water to drink. *And Moses and Aaron* went from the presence of the assembly unto the door of the tabernacle of the congregation, and they *fell upon their faces: and the glory of the* Lord *appeared unto them. And the* Lord *spake unto Moses, saying, Take the rod,* and gather thou the assembly together, thou, and Aaron

thy brother, and *speak ye unto the rock before their eyes; and it shall give forth his water,* and thou shalt bring forth to them water out of the rock: *so thou shalt give the congregation and their beasts drink.* And Moses took the rod from before the LORD, as he commanded him. And Moses and Aaron gathered the congregation together before the rock, and he said unto them, *Hear now, ye rebels; must we fetch you water out of this rock? And Moses lifted up his hand, and with his rod he smote the rock twice: and the water came out abundantly, and the congregation drank, and their beasts also. And the LORD spake unto Moses and Aaron, Because ye believed me not, to sanctify me in the eyes of the children of Israel, therefore ye shall not bring this congregation into the land which I have given them. This* is the water of Meribah; because the children of Israel strove with the LORD, and he was sanctified in them.

—NUMBERS 20:1–13, KJV,
EMPHASIS ADDED

## To consult God for the people

It is the duty of the prophet to consult God on behalf of the people. The purpose of the prophetic office is to bridge the gap of silence between God and mankind. The absence of a prophet means God is quiet to a people, and that could be dangerous. Noah preached a persuasive message of repentance for several years before the flood came.

And it came to pass, when men began to multiply on the face of the earth, and daughters were born unto them, That the sons of God saw the daughters of men that they were fair; and they took them wives of all which they chose.

And the LORD said, *My spirit shall not always strive with man*, for that he also is flesh: yet his days shall be an hundred and twenty years.

There were giants in the earth in those days; and also after that, when the sons of God came in unto the daughters of men, and they bare children to them, the same became mighty men which were of old, men of renown. And *GOD saw that the wickedness of man was great in the earth, and that every imagination of the thoughts of his heart was only evil continually.*

*And it repented the LORD that he had made man on the earth, and it grieved him at his heart. And the LORD said, I will destroy man whom I have created from the face of the earth;* both man, and beast, and the creeping thing, and the fowls of the air; for it repenteth me that I have made them.

*But Noah found grace in the eyes of the LORD.* These are the generations of Noah: *Noah was a just man and perfect in his generations, and Noah walked with God.* And Noah begat three sons, Shem, Ham, and Japheth.

*The earth also was corrupt before God, and the earth was filled with violence.* And God looked upon the earth, and, behold, it was corrupt; *for all flesh had corrupted his way upon the earth.*

> And God said unto Noah, The end of all flesh is come before me; for the earth is filled with violence through them; and, behold, I will destroy them with the earth.
>
> —GENESIS 6:1–13, KJV,
> EMPHASIS ADDED

At this point, God was looking for a prophet to stand in the gap for mankind and the whole earth. Although God found Noah as a man, and sent him to preach a message of repentance, the people did not heed him; hence the flood came and destroyed the whole earth. Then God established Noah and his family to start a new generation of human beings.

> But with thee will I establish my covenant; and thou shalt come into the ark, thou, and thy sons, and thy wife, and thy sons' wives with thee. And of every living thing of all flesh, two of every sort shalt thou bring into the ark, to keep them alive with thee; they shall be male and female. Of fowls after their kind, and of cattle after their kind, of every creeping thing of the earth after his kind, two of every sort shall come unto thee, to keep them alive. And take thou unto thee of all food that is eaten, and thou shalt gather it to thee; and it shall be for food for thee, and for them. Thus did Noah; according to all that God commanded him, so did he.
>
> —GENESIS 6:18–22, KJV

## Combined Ministerial Attributes

The prophetic office can be spread around each of the five-fold ministries. Thus a prophet is not limited to the scope of performing only the functions of a spokesperson as a typical prophet, who only comes to the people when there is a specific message or assignment. The prophet may be called into a combined office of the five-fold ministry, such as operating as a prophet and a shepherd over a denomination—prophet-pastor, prophet-teacher, prophet-evangelist, or prophet-apostle.

Also, every prophet has a specific area of operation besides performing the general prophetic role. Each prophet is called for a purpose and sent on a specific errand. The capability and the unique talents of a prophet reveal his specialized area of operation.

More so the kind of messages received coupled with the divine gifting manifested in his or her ministration identify a prophet as an intercessor, a supplicator, a teacher, a pastor, or an evangelist. Although the gifts usually enhance the existing abilities and the unction that flows through the prophet, the gifts also help to identify some unique roles that are beyond human comprehension.

## The Prophetic Intercessor

A prophetic intercessor is a person who is called to stand in the gap for people with whom he or she does not have a personal contact or a relationship. Based on divine revelation received, an intercessor is often given the burden and assignment to pray for nations, institutions, or individuals. Thus, God shares His burden with the prophet and depends on him to pray until problems are solved and needs are met.

A prophetic intercessor does not draw his or her own prayer list out of pity or sympathy, but seeks the divine will of God and carries out the burden that the Lord has specifically laid on him or her.

Moses as a prophetic intercessor mediated between the children of Israel and the Egyptians. Moses never drew up his own list as to what he thought should be done, but consistently went before the Lord on behalf of Israel.

When the Lord sends me to the nations, my primary assignment is to intercede and do warfare over the nations. The focus of the warfare is to confront the enemy and pull down satanic strongholds, then to arm the nations with the School of Deliverance training so that the body of Christ can experience the joy of salvation.

In order to fulfill this divine mandate, I need to stay in the presence of God and listen carefully, so that my utterance is not that of another prophet, but a mediating prophet in warfare. Often people come against my ministry and attack me because they feel threatened or intimidated; but I am not perturbed, because I am on a divine mission with a mandate to pull down satanic strongholds. I do not go into nations to build a kingdom that moth or rust destroys, but to advance the Christian faith and set the captive free.

Therefore it is pertinent that intercession be made

continuously to release the nation from satanic interferences. Even if the ministers with mega churches attack my mission, I am not moved, because my primary duty is to pull down satanic strongholds through intercessory warfare. Satan can use anybody to interrupt the work of God. We still have a lot of "Pharisees" and "Sadducees" in the church. The Lord showed me how many "men of God" can easily be swayed to act like the high priests that gave up Jesus to Pilate for crucifixion. If the Lord Jesus Christ should rehearse His physical presence on earth again, many ministers and churchgoers would reject Him. As it was in the case of the high priest who was intimidated by the works of the Lord Jesus Christ and his position was threatened, so it is among ministers today.

> And there was one named Barabbas, which lay bound with them that had made insurrection with him, who had committed murder in the insurrection. And the multitude crying aloud began to desire him to do as he had ever done unto them. But Pilate answered them, saying, *Will ye that I release unto you the King of the Jews? For he knew that the chief priests had delivered him for envy. But the chief priests moved the people,* that he should rather release Barabbas unto them.
> —MARK 15:7–11, KJV,
> EMPHASIS ADDED

If everyone would stand in their place of ministry and listen to divine directions, there would be no room for envy and jealousy (the spirit of Korah) to be manifested in the body of Christ.

> *Now Korah*, the son of Izhar, the son of Kohath, the son of Levi, and Dathan and Abiram, the sons of Eliab, and On, the son of Peleth, sons of Reuben, took men: And they rose up before Moses, with certain of the children of Israel, two hundred and fifty princes of the assembly, famous in the congregation, men of renown: And they *gathered themselves together against Moses and against Aaron*, and said unto them, Ye take too much upon you, seeing all the congregation are holy, every one of them, and the LORD is among them: wherefore then lift ye up yourselves above the congregation of the LORD? And when Moses heard it, he fell upon his face.
>
> —NUMBERS 16:1–4, KJV,
> EMPHASIS ADDED

## The Prophetic Supplicator

The prophetic supplicator is an advocate who does not only intercede but also argues a case on behalf of the people. The supplicator discusses issues with the Almighty God based on His divine word and purpose and brings things to God's remembrance. Isaiah 45:11 (KJV) tells us:

> Thus saith the LORD, the Holy One of Israel, and his Maker, Ask me of things to come concerning my sons, and concerning the work of my hands command ye me.

The supplicator hears the voice of the Lord and weighs the judgmental decisions of God and then stands in the gap to intervene on behalf of the people.

Jonah was sent to supplicate for the people of Nineveh, but he refused to play the role of a supplicator; rather he was concerned about his own reputation and wanted God to judge and destroy Nineveh as proclaimed.

> Now the Word of the LORD came to Jonah the second time, saying, *"Arise, go to Nineveh, that great city, and preach to it the message that I tell you."* So Jonah arose and went to Nineveh, according to the Word of the LORD. Now Nineveh was an exceedingly great city, a three-day journey in extent. And Jonah began to enter the city on the first day's walk. Then he cried out and said, "Yet forty days, and Nineveh shall be overthrown!"
>
> So the people of Nineveh believed God, proclaimed a fast, and put on sackcloth, from the greatest to the least of them. Then word came to the king of Nineveh; and he arose from his throne and laid aside his robe, covered himself with sackcloth and sat in ashes. And he cause it to be proclaimed and published throughout Nineveh by the decree of the king and his nobles, saying, let neither man nor beast, herd nor flock, taste anything; do not let them eat, or drink water. But let man and beast be covered with sackcloth, *and cry mightily to God; yes, let every one turn from his evil way and from the violence that is in his hands.* Who can tell if God

will turn and relent, and turn away from His fierce anger, so that we may not perish?

Then God saw their works that they turned form their evil way; and *God relented from the disaster that He had said He would bring upon them, and He did not do it.*

*But it displeased Jonah exceedingly, and he became angry.* So he prayed to the LORD, and said, "Ah, LORD...for I know that You are a gracious and merciful God, slow to anger and abundant in lovingkindness, One who relents from doing harm. Therefore now, O LORD, please take my life from me, for it is better for me to die than to live!"

—JONAH 3:1–10; 4:1–3,
EMPHASIS ADDED

Jonah was able to chat with God at all levels. Even when Jonah was displeased with God, he still had access into His presence to express his feeling.

Similarly, Moses was sent to deliver the children of Israel from the house of bondage. He did not only take them out but also played the role of a supplicator when he reminded God of His divine plan and purpose for Israel. Moses reminded God of who He is and how the surrounding nations would perceive His judgment and condemnation of Israel after bringing them out of the house of bondage.

Then Moses pleaded with the Lord his God, and said: "Lord, why does Your wrath burn hot against Your people whom You have brought out of the land of Egypt with great power and with a mighty hand? Why should the Egyptians speak, and say, 'He brought them out to harm them, to kill them in the mountains, and to consume them from the face of the earth'? Turn from Your fierce wrath, and relent from this harm to Your people. Remember Abraham, Isaac, and Israel, Your servants, to whom You swore by Your own self, and said to them, 'I will multiply your descendants as the stars of heaven; and all this land that I have spoken of I give to your descendants, and they shall inherit it forever.'" So *the Lord relented from the harm which He said He would do to His people.*

—Exodus 32:11–14,
EMPHASIS ADDED

A supplicator is able to cause God to change His decision regarding judgment and condemnation. Both Abraham and Moses were prophets who supplicated at a level that convinced Jehovah God to reverse His decisions.

Abraham was a friend of God and the father of faith. He stood before the Lord and supplicated for Lot and the city of Sodom and Gomorrah.

And the LORD said, "Because *the outcry against Sodom and Gomorrah is great, and because their sin is very grave,* "I will go down now and see whether they have done altogether according to the outcry against it that has come to Me; and if not, I will know."

Then the men turned away from there and went toward Sodom, but Abraham still stood before the LORD. And Abraham came near and said, "*Would*

*You also destroy the righteous with the wicked?*
Suppose there were fifty righteous within the city;
would You also destroy the place and not spare it
for the fifty righteous that were in it? *Far be it from
You to do such a thing as this,* to slay the righteous
with the wicked, so that the righteous should be as
the wicked; far be it from You! *Shall not the Judge of
all the earth do right?"*

—GENESIS 18:20–25,

EMPHASIS ADDED

God demands repentance and not destruction of souls.
Therefore a prophet must stand in the gap and persuade
God to spare the lives of his people (Gen. 20:7)

## The Prophetic Pastor

A prophet-pastor is a person who shepherds the people
besides telling forth His Word. Such a person will often
preach on issues that relate to the plans and purposes of
God based on revelatory knowledge. The sermon often
focuses on revelatory knowledge and interpretation of
prophetic events.

The prophet-pastor is sensitive to what the Lord is
saying to His people in the congregation and the body of
Christ as a whole. The prophet-pastor guards his people
against the evils of the times that are likely to becloud the
neighborhood and the territory in which they live.

The prophet-pastor does not just preach sermons or
practice routine duty or preaching, but he listens to the

heartbeat of God. He or she perceives the burden on the heart of God for a particular time and season while preparing sermonic messages.

The prophetic-pastor does not feed the flock with snacks for excitement or any meal to fill up the belly, but with a meal that nourishes, builds, and strengthens both the individual and the members of congregation as one body of Christ.

A prophet-pastor does not necessarily stand in the pulpit to prophecy "thus says the Lord," but from his or her teaching and utterances, it will be clear that the pastor is releasing fresh bread like manna from heaven. The reputation of the prophetic word flows like a spring of fresh water in the character and behavior of the presenter and in the lives of the recipients.

## The Prophetic Teacher

The prophet being God's spokesman will always function around the plans and purposes of God for every season. His or her teaching will be related to prophetic mysteries and events. A prophetic teacher is a prophet who also operates in the office of a teacher. Elisha was a prophet and a teacher. He taught in the school of the prophets.

As a prophet, Moses received the laws from God but did not just hand them over to the people. Moses was also mandated to teach the people to apply the laws of God to their daily endeavors. In the book of Leviticus and Deuter-onomy, Moses taught the children of God to practice the laws of God. The Ten Commandments were interpreted and simplified for understanding and application.

Similarly, the prophet-teacher is expected to bring the Word to the knowledge of the people to enable them to understand the laws of God and practice them effectively. The prophet-teacher is also responsible for watching over the seasons that the Word of the Lord comes into practical manifestation.

In the days when the Virgin Mary conceived by the Holy Ghost the baby Jesus, the prophets were asleep and the Levites and priests had lost their connections with God, so they were no longer in tune with the seasons of divine manifestations.

Instead of discerning and accepting the conception of the Virgin Mary, they rather persecuted her. Therefore the Lord revealed the mystery to some wise men from the eastern countries. The wise men believed the birth of the baby Jesus and went on a journey that gave an indication to King Herod that a new King had been born. Of course Herod became intimidated and threatened, so he made an attempt to destroy the newborn King.

The prophetic-teacher has the responsibility to watch over the seasons and teach us to honor prophetic manifestations.

## The Prophetic Evangelist

Some prophets also operate as evangelists. They have a burden for the salvation of souls. John the Baptist was a prophet who also functioned as an evangelist. His message was focused on repentance. Jonah was a prophet-evangelist who was sent to deliver the message of repentance to the people of Nineveh.

Not all evangelists are prophets, neither are all prophets evangelists. A prophet-evangelist is not fulfilled until souls are saved; the messages that he or she receives demand his involvement in evangelism. Jonah was sent as a prophet-evangelist to Nineveh so that the people of Nineveh would repent and change their ways.

The burden of a prophet operating in the office of an evangelist is strongly based on how to save souls and deliver the lost from bondage. The utterances that flow from the belly of a prophet-evangelist are persuasive and encouraging toward repentance. A prophet-evangelist seeks divine direction and instruction that enables him to touch the heart of the sin-sick soul. The burden is to set the captives free and release those in bondage. The message may contain a threat to the stubborn hearts that reject the truth, yet it will still pass on the wave of the love of Jesus and the importance of His death on the cross. God does not take delight in the death of a sinner, so judgment and condemnation is not a song on the lips of an evangelist, but the cry of repentance and intercession for the innocent living in the midst of evil.

> There was a man of the Pharisees, named Nico-
> demus, a ruler of the Jews: The same came to Jesus
> by night, and said unto him, Rabbi, we know that
> thou art a teacher come from God: for no man can

do these miracles that thou doest, except God be with him. Jesus answered and said unto him, Verily, verily, I say unto thee, Except a man be born again, he cannot see the kingdom of God. Nicodemus saith unto him, *How can a man be born when he is old? can he enter the second time into his mother's womb, and be born? Jesus answered, Verily, verily, I say unto thee, Except a man be born of water and of the Spirit, he cannot enter into the kingdom of God. That which is born of the flesh is flesh; and that which is born of the Spirit is spirit.* Marvel not that I said unto thee, Ye must be born again. The wind bloweth where it listeth, and thou hearest the sound thereof, but canst not tell whence it cometh, and whither it goeth: so is every one that is born of the Spirit. Nicodemus answered and said unto him, *How can these things be?* Jesus answered and said unto him, Art thou a master of Israel, and knowest not these things? Verily, verily, I say unto thee, We speak that we do know, and testify that we have seen; and ye receive not our witness. If I have told you *earthly things*, and ye believe not, how shall ye believe, if I tell you of *heavenly things?* And no man hath ascended up to heaven, but he that came down from heaven, even the Son of man which is in heaven. And *as Moses lifted up the serpent in the wilderness, even so must the Son of man be lifted up: That whosoever believeth in him should not perish, but have everlasting life. For God so loved the world, that he gave his only begotten Son, that whosoever believeth in him should not perish, but have everlasting life. For God sent not his Son into the world to condemn the world; but that the world through him might be saved. He that believeth on him is not condemned: but he that believeth not is condemned already, because he hath not believed in the name of the only begotten Son of God.* And this is the condemnation, that light is come into the world, and men loved darkness rather than light, because their deeds were evil. For every one that doeth evil hateth the light, neither cometh to the light, lest his deeds should be reproved. But he that doeth truth cometh to the light, that his deeds may be made manifest, that they are wrought in God.

… He that cometh from above is above all: he that is of the earth is earthly, and speaketh of the earth: he that cometh from heaven is above all. And what he hath seen and heard, that he testifieth; and no man receiveth his testimony. He that hath received his testimony hath set to his seal that God is true. *For he whom God hath sent speaketh the words of God: for God giveth not the Spirit by measure unto him.* The Father loveth the Son, and hath given all things into his hand. He that believeth on the Son hath everlasting life: and he that believeth not the Son shall not see life; but the wrath of God abideth on him.

—JOHN 3:1–21, 31–36, KJV,
EMPHASIS ADDED

The following are some of the prophets whose calling were combined with other ministries:

- Moses the Prophet-Leader and Supplicator: a Prophetic Leader

- Joshua the Prophet-Leader and Warrior: a Prophetic Warrior

- Samuel the Prophet-Priest and Judge: a Prophetic Judge

- Isaiah the Prophet-Priest and Poet: a Prophetic-Priest

- Daniel the Prophet-Counselor and Intercessor: a Prophetic Intercessor

- Elijah the Prophet-Warrior: a Prophetic Warrior

- Elisha the Prophet-Teacher and Administrator: a Prophetic Deliverance Administrator

- Jeremiah the Prophet-Judge (The warning prophet): a Prophetic Judge

- Ezekiel the Prophet-Priest: a Prophetic-Priest

## Chapter 6

# THE CHANNELS OF COMMUNICATION

THE LORD COMMUNICATES with the prophet through various channels. There are different channels of communication in the spiritual realm just as there are in the physical, emotional, and secular realms. The realms of communication are very crucial to the prophetic office. Without spiritual channels of communication, it would almost be impossible for man to connect to God, even though God always devises supernatural means to reach out to mankind. That would mean that unless God came down to visit us on earth, we would not have the opportunity to make contact with Him at all. Otherwise, anytime He came down to us, all the prophets in the world would have to queue up to take turns to enter into His presence. Not only so, but God would have to visit different nations at different times in order to reach out to us.

However, God is omnipresent and the only wise God of yesterday, today, and forever, so He is able to reach out to mankind in all the earth simultaneously, and we can all hear him at once if we choose to listen and accommodate Him. Although we might hear Him differently, according to our individual understanding, language, cultural, and traditional background, we will hear Him if we pay attention to Him.

Once, one of my prayer partners, Brother Lambert, and I had a burden to pray for ministers of the gospel to obey the Lord and to preach messages that would advance the kingdom of God. Every weekend we would fast and pray for ministers all around the world to preach the true message that would solve problems and meet the needs of congregation members. After a period of time, we decided to test some of the revelations we had received. In order for us to achieve specific results relating to our prayers and expectations, we began to utter specific prayers that would enable us to identify the responses that the Lord released unto us.

Every weekend we prayed that God would reveal to us His plans for a particular weekend. We prayed that God would change the messages that were contrary to His will so that all the ministers scheduled to preach on a particular Sunday would present the pure Word of the Lord.

The Lord then showed us how He desires to meet the needs of His children at our gatherings. He showed us how it is His divine will to give His children specific instructions that are for problem solving in our daily endeavors. Then He also showed us how many ministers do not stay still in His presence to listen or take instructions from Him.

Based on the revelations received, we decided to pray over the churches and also focus on certain denominations in a particular community. We also scheduled a visit to three churches per Sunday for a period of time. Our aim was to see how ministers respond to divine leadership.

On the first Sunday, the episode was the same in all the three churches we visited. We visited two Pentecostal denominations and an Evangelical church. We had prayed that the pastors would specifically indicate that, "This is not the message I had prepared to preach, but the Lord is giving me another message as I prepare to mount the pulpit." Behold, the ministers mounted up to the pulpit and began to make the exact statements as we had prayed. Also, the messages were similar and the topics, though not framed in the same manner, meant the same. The contents of the messages were just the same, but presented differently because each of them did not prepare for the new message that the Lord prompted them to preach. Interestingly, they all used the same Scripture as the foundation of their message.

On the second Sunday, we noted how some ministers

struggled to preach their sermons, as they fumbled and made several mistakes, which some of them promptly corrected, and some just ignored. It was easy to detect a common language from ministers that were not submissive to authority and obedient to the prompting of the Holy Spirit. In some of the churches where the ministers struggled to preach their ready-made sermons, almost half of the congregation fell asleep while some church members disrupted the service with their movements.

In one of the churches, a pastor was pleased to announce that the particular message he had for that Sunday was a popular request, because the tapes for that message sold out the last time it was preached. This pastor did not preach any sermon and did not repeat the message either. He began telling stories of his beautiful trip to some places and his expectations and dreams of new projects. That Sunday morning was wasted, yet the congregation cheered and celebrated freely without hearing a life-changing sermon, a solution-oriented sermon.

That Sunday's sermon was focused on the pastor himself: Christ was absent from his lips, Jesus was missing in his language, and the Holy Spirit was bottled and decorated like a flowerpot on the altar. And the congregation celebrated the pastor because they praised every statement he made with great excitement. Hero worship was the act of the day.

For the next three Sundays, we observed the manner in which each minister responded to divine prompting instantly or sluggishly. We also noted how some of them ignored and snubbed the presence of the Lord. We observed how God speaks to each person differently in a language that they would understand. Thus, while some of the ministers explained that the Lord spoke to them, some claimed to have seen a vision, and some felt a prompting, while one particular pastor felt the need to narrate a dream he once had, and that changed the content of the message he had prepared to preach.

As we prayed and tested the spiritual connections that individual ministers had with the Lord, we realized how the Lord splashes His Word unto us like showers of rain. Each person receives the rainwater according to his or her understanding and expectation. Some receive the rain water in a bucket, some dig a drainage ditch to collect the water, and some open their mouths to drink directly from the rainfall, while others choose to seek refuge under an umbrella and others bath in the rain or wash their hands with it.

When the Lord releases a revelation, those who are sleeping may receive it in a form of a dream; those who are awake may hear it directly in their ears or see it in a vision; those who are alert may smell it in a form of an intuition or perception; and some may fall into a trance. Those who may be praying at the time of the release may suddenly begin to prophesy. A person who operates in the gift of prophecy may be carried into a state of ecstasy and begin to speak out unconsciously, while a person who operates in the office of a prophet will receive the word fully and present it consciously. Sometimes the prophet may receive a word, a statement, or a picture either by hearing or seeing or perceiving.

However, as soon as the person opens the mouth to speak, words begin to pour out of him or her as though a tap of water has been opened. Sometimes when a person who is rich in the Word of God and well connected in prayer opens the mouth to speak, it is as though a floodgate of a river has been opened. Such a person speaks with clarity, and the words that flow out of them are full of precious stones like silver, gold, beryl, or onyx.

Also, the blessings of fresh water flow with peace, joy, healing, deliverance, and satisfaction that attract a praise-worship celebration. When a fresh water blessing is poured out through a prophetic word, there is a flow of knowledge, wisdom, and understanding. There is no room for confusion and anxiety unless the recipients are prone to worry and anxiety. Individual persons who are not stable in the Word of God are not able to receive and drink from the rivers of living waters.

> Blessed is the man that walketh not in the counsel of the ungodly, nor standeth in the way of sinners, nor sitteth in the seat of the scornful. But his delight is in the law of the LORD; and in his law doth he meditate day and night. *And he shall be like a tree planted by the rivers of water, that bringeth forth his fruit in his season; his leaf also shall not wither; and whatsoever he doeth shall prosper.*
>
> *The ungodly are not so: but are like the chaff which the wind driveth away.* Therefore the ungodly shall

not stand in the judgment, nor sinners in the congregation of the righteous. For the LORD knoweth the way of the righteous: but the way of the ungodly shall perish.

—PSALM 1, KJV,

EMPHASIS ADDED

Individual persons who are anxious for the prophetic word do not usually stay still to study Scriptures. Such anxious persons are not able to hear the word that will build them up in the Lord. They attend fellowship meetings and conferences with the intention to seek prophetic words and personal ministration. Prophetic-anxious persons do not know the importance of Bible studies. Anxiety causes a person to fret and run around town seeking a prophetic word, but it does nothing to build a personal Christian life and relationship with the Lord.

Hence, prophetic-anxious persons receive a multitude of prophecies from different people that seem to clash and confuse the mind. Prophetic-anxious persons are porous and vulnerable. They gulp anything and swallow everything that is called prophecy. Because they are usually poor in spirit due to lack of knowledge of Scripture, they absorb everything including that which contaminates.

The foundational channel of communication that everyone should seek is the written Word of God—the Scriptures. The Scripture is the foundation of divine knowledge. When you know what the Bible says, no prophet can deceive you, and no voice can confuse you. If you do not know what the Scripture says, it is easy to sway from the truth and follow a prophetic voice that may be confusing because the interpretation is wrong. It is important that you make a conscious effort to build up your Christian life, then it will be easy for you to flow in the blessings that God has for you.

> Wherefore, my beloved, as ye have always obeyed, not as in my presence only, but now much more in my absence, work out your own salvation with fear and trembling. For it is God which worketh in you both to will and to do of *his* good pleasure.
> —PHILIPPIANS 2:12–13, KJV,
> EMPHASIS ADDED

Although a message may truly come from the Lord, lack of knowledge could infuse falsehood into it. Sometimes the message is true, but the channel is corrupted. An ungodly lifestyle of a person can easily corrupt the prophetic word. Persons who are vulnerable or susceptible to the works of the flesh such as lust, sexual sin, pride, ego, and anger easily open doors for the enemy to interfere with the prophetic word.

> Of these things put them in remembrance, charging them before the Lord that they strive not about words to no profit, but to the subverting of the hearers. Study to shew thyself approved unto God, a workman that needeth not to be ashamed, rightly dividing the word of truth. But shun profane and vain babblings: for they will increase unto more ungodliness. And their word will eat as doth a canker: of whom is Hymenaeus and Philetus; Who

concerning the truth have erred, saying that the resurrection is past already; and overthrow the faith of some. Nevertheless the foundation of God standeth sure, having this seal, The Lord knoweth them that are his. And, Let every one that nameth the name of Christ depart from iniquity. But in a great house there are not only vessels of gold and of silver, but also of wood and of earth; and some to honour, and some to dishonour. If a man therefore purge himself from these, he shall be a vessel unto honour, sanctified, and meet for the master's use, and prepared unto every good work. Flee also youthful lusts: but follow righteousness, faith, charity, peace, with them that call on the Lord out of a pure heart. But foolish and unlearned questions avoid, knowing that they do gender strifes. And the servant of the Lord must not strive; but be gentle unto all men, apt to teach, patient, In meekness instructing those that oppose themselves; if God peradventure will give them repentance to the acknowledging of the truth; And that they may recover themselves out of the snare of the devil, who are taken captive by him at his will.

—2 TIMOTHY 2:14–26, KJV

Therefore, it is pertinent that the individuals who operate in the prophetic must study the Scriptures. They must allow the written Word of God to fill their hearts and flow like a river in their personal character. By so doing they will avoid corruption but keep the prophetic word with its interpretation pure and holy.

The channels of divine communication include the revelatory avenues that are listed below:

**The word of wisdom**

The word of wisdom is the ability to know what the future holds. It is a prediction of the plans and purposes of God for mankind or a people or a nation. Most of the Old Testament prophets predicted the future of Israel and the promises of God for His people and the other nations.

More often than not, prophetic revelation operates with the word of wisdom. Daniel was a prophet who predicted the jet age and the development of technology (the world powers and political kingdoms—socialism, communism, and capitalism). Today, over one hundred prophecies foretold by Daniel have been noted as fulfilled. (See Daniel 7.)

For instance, in November 2006, when I was invited by a church to hold a Mentoring and Leadership conference, the Lord showed me many revelations to confirm that He had heard the cry of the people of Guyana. As an answer to the prayer of the body of Christ in Guyana, the Lord would release a type of revival that would cut across all facets of the nation's existence.

Thus the Lord would release a revival that will bring forth the healing of the nation's economy and bring forth abundance of wealth in the agricultural sector. The natural resources of the land would gain a place of importance on the world market. The mineral resources like gold, silver, and bauxite would be restored unto the nations. The social infrastructure would be improved. There would be employment opportunities in the nation, and the socio-economic status of the nation would improve as a result of the revival.

The Lord also mentioned the fact that both the ungodly and the righteous would contribute their wealth and substances to the building of the nation's socio-economic development, and that the Christians would inherit the wealth of the ungodly and they would prosper as a result of the revival of the economy.

Following that prophetic utterance on the last day of the conference in November 2006, the Lord gave me a mandate to organize an intercessory prayer for the nation of Guyana. In February 2007, we held meetings in various parts of Guyana to usher in the revival. By the end of the year 2007, there was a great change in the economy of Guyana.

When I returned to Guyana in February 2008, I could not recognize some parts of the nation. Many roads have been reconstructed and traffic lights have been installed. Individuals have been able to renovate and remodel their homes. New buildings are springing up to replace the old ones. The economy of the nation of Guyana is fast improving.

This is an example of a word of wisdom that was spoken over a nation and it was fulfilled within a short period of time. In fact the manifestation of the Word of the Lord is still in process as the revival has just begun.

**The word of knowledge**

The word of knowledge is the ability to know the present disposition of a situation or person without having a prior knowledge of it. It is the ability to perceive and fore-tell a live situation concerning a person or a place through the power of the Holy Spirit. God is omnipresent and all knowing; He usually releases information to prophets by supernatural means. The word of knowledge is one of the unique channels through which God speaks to and through the prophets since biblical days.

I was invited to minister in a church in New Jersey. As soon as I sat in the chair allotted to me, I noticed a gentleman at the far end of the front row. The gentleman looked like a bishop. In fact I saw the man decorated in a bishop's regalia and a hat, but in the physical, the man was simply dressed up in a black suit.

During personal ministrations, the man was one of the elders that assisted at the altar. Usually, I would bless the people who assist me at the end of ministration. When I started ministering to the gentleman, the Lord showed me that he had lost much wealth and properties, and that everything would be restored to him, because he had repented and submitted himself for restoration. I also mentioned the revelation of the bishop's apparel and the abundance of gold that the Lord had given to him. I saw so much gold that I called him the gold man. Unknown to me, everything I said had already taken place in the gentleman's life. After his predicament, he submitted himself for restoration in that church. Hence, the Lord visited him with the message of healing and restoration through the word of knowledge.

## The discernment of spirits

Discerning of spirits is the ability to know the type of spirit operating in a person or at a place. Through supernatural means, the prophet is able to discern spiritual activities in both the positive and the negative realms. The prophet needs discerning of spirits to determine the presence of God and the voice he or she is relating to at any point in time.

Many people have been cajoled by evil spirits because they are not able to discern between genuine and deceptive spirits. Unfortunately, many ignorant churchgoers think that the practice of consulting psychics and palmistry or indulging in clairvoyance is an alternative means of seeking the attention of God.

In 1998 I was invited to minister in a church in London. When I mounted the pulpit, there was a young lady in the front who started manifesting as she tried to prophesy. Immediately the Lord opened my eyes to see the kind of spirit in her. She was all wrapped up by a serpent, and seated on top of her head was the head of a snake. The serpent's mouth was wide opened ready to swallow whatever message I had to share.

So I ordered the young lady to sit down, having discerned that she was an agent of Satan and a false prophetess. During ministration I tried to cast out the serpent spirit from her, but the bishop of the church stopped me.

According to him, the serpent lady was a nice person whose prophecies had been helpful to his ministry. When I began to explain about the lady, the bishop got upset.

At the end of the service, some persons confirmed that the woman had a live serpent in her house and she practiced divination for the bishop. She was also rich and had houses, one of which the bishop resided in. Soon after that incident, the bishop was busted and the secret of his deceptive ministerial dealings was exposed to the public.

Recently some ladies visited our ministry at the Overcomers' House. When I entered the auditorium, I noticed two snakeheads and a monkey seated on a shoulder. I said, "What are these two women doing here? Have they come to test power or suck up power in the house?" The Lord said for me to ignore them and focus on my ministration. They had come to seek help.

At the end of the service, they were brought into my office for counseling. Instead of humbling themselves, they introduced themselves as prophetesses and worshipers. "Wow, I muttered!! What a deception!" They began to narrate how the Lord sent them to prophesy to some individuals and they were resisted, hence they were hurt and disappointed.

As usual, I ignored their boastful pride and began to expose their indulgence in the horoscope and prophetic fictions. They later confessed that they had gone to seek help from some individuals and they were given some oil to rub on their bodies. They actually tried to blame another person for contaminating them. They would still not tell the truth about their involvement in spiritism. It is a case of a prophet seeking prophecies. They actually wanted me to tell them what the Lord had to tell them regarding the people who resisted them from prophesying.

Sometimes when I go a church, the pastors are quick to introduce certain individuals to me as prophets or prophetesses. Instantly I will discern the spirit behind their utterances to be misleading. Some of them are genuine, yet they focus too much on delivering the prophetic word without seeking to develop their Christian life and spiritual strength.

## Vision (opened eyes and closed eyes vision)

Vision is the ability to perceive the things that pertain to the spirit realm either with the eyes opened or closed. Some prophets are seers. They are able to see into the spirit realm with eyes opened or closed. They make pronouncements by stating what they see happening in the spirit realm; they see things that are either already in process or about to take place. Through a vision a prophet can relay events from the past, through the present, and into the future.

Sometimes when I am teaching the Word, preaching, or ministering to an individual, something like a huge television screen suddenly appears before me. On the television screen will appear current and past events taking place either in the immediate world around the people present, the city, or nation in which I am ministering at the time or in the life of an individual that is receiving ministration. This manner of revelation can be described as an open vision.

An open vision is not a trance, because one is conscious but has the ability to see into the spirit realm. In the case of a trance, one is usually lost in thought and unconscious. In a trance one suddenly slips away from the physical realm into the spiritual realm in a moment of unconsciousness.

An open vision is a strong prophetic ability that enables a person operating in the prophetic office to discern the things of the spirit (good or evil) while he or she is alert and conscious of their surroundings. It is another realm of the seer. The seer has the ability to see into the present and future. A seer does not need to close the eyes to see into the spirit realm.

## Intuition

This is a state of having an immediate insight into a matter without prior knowledge or thought of it. It is a spontaneous apprehension of something that is about to take place or is already happening in the spiritual or physical realm.

Intuition is a spontaneous sensitivity to the Holy Spirit and also to things that are spiritual. Intuition is the ability to have instant perception or immediate insight into matters by premonition that is motivated by the supernatural.

Intuition is another form of the word of knowledge. When something is about to happen or something is going wrong physically, a person who operates in this gift will suddenly feel like praying or go into a place to intervene in the matter.

A person with this gift will often act like an extrovert and ruthless. If the person has no self-control, he or she will act in a manner that could easily offend people. But if the person is mature and has self-control, he or she takes over situations with the application of Scripture and wisdom, so that their good works will not become an offense to onlookers.

## Perception

Perception is a type of spiritual intelligence. It is an ability to recognize things that have spiritual connotation. It is also the ability to grasp the meaning of things that pertain to the supernatural realm and discern the information connected to it. It is a premonition that something is about to happen, thus to know a situation by smelling or sensing it in the spiritual realm.

Daniel had perception of things that took place in the spiritual realm. Even as a teenage prophet, Daniel was able to perceive the spiritual connotation of the food that was served in the king's palace. Hence, he refused to partake of it.

Intuition is a gift that functions in an extrovert while perception is a gift that operates well with introverts. People who operate in the realms of perceiving take their time to make a decision and do apply a lot of tactics to intervene in matters that could be delicate or dangerous.

Although an intuitive person is also acting on the

prompting of the Holy Spirit, his or her inability to calm down and think through the revelation may cause pain or bruise the individuals involved.

People who are susceptible to the work of the flesh are easily offended even by the move of God to save and deliver them from evil. Lack of self-control can make a person burst out in wrath in the middle of a worship service where the Holy Spirit is moving and blessing people.

People who are proud and egocentric have no respect for prophetic intuition or perception. Such individuals can react and attack any move made to salvage or deliver somebody from evil.

## Hearing

Besides hearing with the physical ears, some prophets also have the faculty of hearing spiritual sounds from God supernaturally. Prophetic hearing is the ability to grasp or perceive the voice of God and respond to it spontaneously and accordingly.

## Trance

A trance is a state of dreaming while a person is awake but partly unconscious. Sometimes a person in a trance feels lost or suspended in the air, as though being raptured. It is a vicarious state of mind with an ecstatic feeling. Also, a trance is a sleeplike state without response to stimuli. Peter entered a trance that revealed the need for him to accept and minister to the Gentiles—Cornelius and his household.

### Prophetic dream

A dream is a state of perceiving an event or visualizing dramatic activities while asleep. A dream can be a replay of things that are in action or things that have already happened or things that are yet to come.

A prophetic dream is the ability to dream the reality of events that are present, past, or about to happen. A dream is prophetic because the event concerned is unfolded just as it was revealed.

All dreams are not prophetic, but some are, because the prophet is also able to submit himself or herself to the relaying of the events that follows the revelation. Joseph was a prophetic dreamer. He humbly walked in the fear of God and submitted himself to the challenges of the times and seasons that were connected to the unfolding of his dreams. Despite the persecutions he went through, Joseph stayed calm and maintained his relationship with God.

I am not a dreamer, so whenever I sleep and wake up with a strong memory of a dream and am also motivated to pray over it, I know it is a revelation from God. In order for me to judge if the dream is a revelation or not, I will have to examine my thoughts before I went to sleep. I will also check my feelings and conversation of an issue to make sure that the thoughts in my mind did not filter into my sleep and become a dream.

If I go to bed hungry, I will dream of my favorite food. So when I wake up, I do not need to question the fact that I ate a delicious meal in my dream. All I need to do to solve the problem is cook that delicious meal to satisfy my conscience.

Also, if I have to perform a duty and choose to sleep instead, my dream will focus on that unfinished assignment. From this, I am able to deduce when a dream is an overflow of my thoughts or a revelation from God. Praise God, any dream that is a revelation has often been fulfilled with twenty-four hours or a week to a month of receiving it.

## The Sensory Organs

The prophetic channels of communication are connected to the sensory organs. The Holy Spirit operates on human's sensory organs, and people in the prophetic ministry are susceptible to the Holy Spirit. The sensory organs' connections are adapted as such:

- Eyes to see—vision
- Ears to hear—voice
- Nose to smell—perception
- Mouth to speak—utterance
- Heart to feel—intuition
- Nerves to sense—sensation
- Mind to dream—trance

Chapter 7

# THE PROPHETIC WORD, THE PROPHETIC LANGUAGE

THE PROPHETIC MESSAGE is a word from God delivered by His errand person. The prophetic word may reveal the plans and purposes of God or the displeasure of the Lord. The fact that a message is coming from the Lord does not mean it will be all positive. Sometimes, when a message has a negative connotation, people refuse to pay attention to it.

Once I was in a church where people who have a prophetic word were expected to come forward and receive the microphone to speak. During one of the services, a young man came forward along with others. When the young man began to prophesy, the leaders of the church became displeased with his utterance, so the moderator took away the microphone. Part of the young man's utterance included, "I will judge this nation. I will start my judgment from this very place with leaders who walk in disobedience to my word."

In order to nullify the young man's prophecy, one of the church leaders jumped up and went for the microphone. He began to praise the leaders of the church and the greatness of the nation. The congregation received the leader's positive words with the response of "Amen" and also clapped their hands to honor the positive message. After this episode, a series of sermons was preached to thwart the young man's prophetic word.

Of course the young man was frustrated and discouraged. He was called and rebuked by several of the leaders after the church service. However, since the Word of the Lord never fails, the prophetic message that was rejected came to pass. A few months later, the leadership of the government was overthrown and the nation came under the iron hand of a military dictatorship. The church concerned also struggled with its leadership. People then remembered the message that was rejected. Several years later circumstances took that leadership out of office. However, nobody deemed it fit to apologize to the gentleman.

Although people are curious about what God has to say to them, the prophetic language has not always been palatable to the ears of the listener. From the time of Noah in the sixth chapter of the book of Genesis, mankind has often felt uncomfortable with the prophetic language. Mankind has often refused the prophetic word because, like in the case of Cain, the word is often a warning against sin or repercussion of sin. Although people expect the prophetic language to be positive and aromatic, it is rather a mixture of romance and rebuke, among other things.

More often than not, people are fond of aromatic and inspirational prophecies that cuddle them into a state of ecstasy: "My children, my children, I love you, I love you. I will never leave nor forsake you." Many people are not aware of the fact that the same Scripture that offers love also prunes the ones that God loves. The same Scripture that advocates love also declares that God will be honest to those who will be honest to Him, and shrewd to the devious.

Psalm 18:24–26, (KJV) tells us:

> Therefore hath the LORD recompensed me according to my righteousness, according to the cleanness of my hands in his eyesight. With the merciful thou wilt shew thyself merciful; with an upright man thou wilt shew thyself upright; With the pure thou wilt shew thyself pure; and with the froward thou wilt shew thyself froward.

Therefore, God will not sing a song of love to us when we are stiff-necked in our disobedience. He will chastise us and then draw us with the cords of love.

Hebrews 12:5–8, (KJV) states:

And ye have forgotten the exhortation which spea-keth unto you as unto children, My son, despise not thou the chastening of the Lord, nor faint when thou art rebuked of him: For whom the Lord loveth he chasteneth, and scourgeth every son whom he receiveth. If ye endure chastening, God dealeth with you as with sons; for what son is he whom the father chasteneth not? But if ye be without chastisement, whereof all are partakers, then are ye bastards, and not sons.

This chapter discusses the prophetic word and the language that is often used that has been misunderstood by both believers and non-churchgoers.

## The positive word

The prophetic word is destiny oriented. It reveals the plans and purposes of God for every human being and a nation. When God is pleased with a person, a people, or a nation, the prophetic word would reveal the loving-kindness of God's heart. The prophetic word has several attributes. The prophetic word is progressive; therefore, it is spoken and written for the existence of mankind.

## The progressive word

The Word of God functions in a continuous motion. It is meant for all human beings from generation to genera-tion. The Word of God is ever active and has no room for stagnancy. It is progressive because it has an impact on every human being created in His image and on all crea-tures. Because the Word of God is progressive, all things shall pass away; but His Word will continue to remain active and effective in heaven and on earth.

The prophet that delivers the word will pass away, but the Word of God will remain the same. Noah and all the prophets that delivered the Word of the Lord have departed this world, but the prophetic message that they spoke is still with us today. The prophetic word is progressively everlasting as Scripture declares that all things shall pass away but His Word would ever remain the same.

Matthew 24:34–35 (KJV) declares:

> Verily I say unto you, This generation shall not pass, till all these things be fulfilled. Heaven and earth shall pass away, but my words shall not pass away.

The Word of the Lord is like a seed, so it has the ability to germinate, grow, and flourish (Psalm 1). The developmental process of the Word of God makes the prophetic language fit into every generation in human existence. Whether one accepts the prophetic language or not, one's attitude does not affect what God intends to do in a particular season.

> For as the rain cometh down, and the snow from heaven, and returneth not thither, but watereth the earth, and maketh it bring forth and bud, that it may give seed to the sower, and bread to the eater: So shall my word be that goeth forth out of my mouth: it shall not return unto me void, but it shall accomplish that which I please, and it shall prosper in the thing whereto I sent it.
> —ISAIAH 55:10–11, KJV

The prophetic language is the onus that carries the weight of the prophetic word. It is the language that distinguishes the prophetic word from the words of mankind. The prophetic language has a unique impetus that stands out clearly from the day-to-day expression of human beings. Sometimes you know that a person is not speaking of himself or herself because of the difference in the language of expression. When you are familiar with certain people, it is easy to tell when they start to do the uncommon things and to speak in a certain way that they would not be able to when they are in their consciousness.

When the prophetic word is released, it goes out as a seed or a sword, depending on the purpose for which it is released. When the prophetic word is sent out as a seed, a person who receives it will begin to grow and develop in a manner that will fashion their life into fulfillment.

Similarly, if the prophetic word is released to affect a child's destiny, that word will grow with the child. The child's life shall be shaped by the prophetic word as the child grows up until the word fits into his or her destiny in time and in season.

Similarly, if a prophetic word is released as a sword, it will go forth to confront the enemy and fight battles for deliverance. The word goes forth to disarm the enemy from intrusion and interference with the righteous. The prophetic deliverance word will continue the action of warfare until the battle is won.

> For the Word of God is quick, and powerful, and sharper than any twoedged sword, piercing even to the dividing asunder of soul and spirit, and of the joints and marrow, and is a discerner of the thoughts and intents of the heart.
>
> —HEBREWS 4:12, KJV

The Word of God is never stagnant, although the recipient may be stagnant because of lack of understanding or lack of comprehension. Even if humans continue to live and walk in disobedience, the Word of God will always be actively progressive. God will continue to move His purposes around until someone responds and says, "Here am I, send me."

> Then flew one of the seraphims unto me, having a live coal in his hand, which he had taken with the tongs from off the altar: And he laid it upon my mouth, and said, Lo, this hath touched thy lips; and thine iniquity is taken away, and thy sin purged. *Also I heard the voice of the Lord, saying, Whom shall I send, and who will go for us? Then said I, Here am I; send me.*
>
> —ISAIAH 6:6–8, KJV,
> EMPHASIS ADDED

**The spoken word**

The prophetic word is a declaration of the intention of God. God reveals the secret of His heart to the prophet, and the prophet declares or pronounces it unto the people.

The Word of the Lord must be spoken for there to

be a manifestation. Unless the word is spoken, nothing happens. In Genesis 1, God spoke creation into being. Once the Word of God is declared through the prophetic, an action will begin to take place in the spiritual realm. The Holy Spirit will start to work on the word that has been spoken. Like a seed, the fertile land or heart will receive the word, and then growth and germination will take place until the time or season is ripe for manifestation and fulfillment.

**The written word**

It is the spoken Word of God that is also written for the remembrance of His creatures and for historical records. The prophetic word is progressive, therefore God mandated His prophets to write it down. There have been times when the children of Israel had forgotten the commandments of God, and the written word has been a point of reminder.

Second Kings 22:1-20 (KJV) tells us of one of those times.

> Josiah was eight years old when he began to reign, and he reigned thirty and one years in Jerusalem. And his mother's name was Jedidah, the daughter of Adaiah of Boscath. And he did that which was right in the sight of the LORD, and walked in all the way of David his father, and turned not aside to the right hand or to the left.
>
> And it came to pass in the eighteenth year of king Josiah, that the king sent Shaphan the son of Azaliah, the son of Meshullam, the scribe, to the house of

the LORD, saying, Go up to Hilkiah the high priest, that he may sum the silver which is brought into the house of the LORD, which the keepers of the door have gathered of the people: And let them deliver it into the hand of the doers of the work, that have the oversight of the house of the LORD: and let them give it to the doers of the work which is in the house of the LORD, to repair the breaches of the house, Unto carpenters, and builders, and masons, and to buy timber and hewn stone to repair the house. Howbeit there was no reckoning made with them of the money that was delivered into their hand, because they dealt faithfully.

And Hilkiah the high priest said unto Shaphan the scribe, *I have found the book of the law in the house of the LORD. And Hilkiah gave the book to Shaphan, and he read it.* And Shaphan the scribe came to the king, and brought the king word again, and said, Thy servants have gathered the money that was found in the house, and have delivered it into the hand of them that do the work, that have the oversight of the house of the LORD. And Shaphan the scribe shewed the king, saying, *Hilkiah the priest hath delivered me a book. And Shaphan read it before the king.*

And it came to pass, *when the king had heard the words of the book of the law, that he rent his clothes._* And the king commanded Hilkiah the priest, and Ahikam the son of Shaphan, and Achbor the son of Michaiah, and Shaphan the scribe, and Asahiah a servant of the king's, saying, *Go ye, enquire of the LORD for me, and for the people, and for all Judah,*

*concerning the words of this book that is found:*
*for great is the wrath of the* LORD *that is kindled*
*against us, because our fathers have not hearkened*
*unto the words of this book, to do according unto all*
*that which is written concerning us.* So Hilkiah the
priest, and Ahikam, and Achbor, and Shaphan, and
Asahiah, *went unto Huldah the prophetess,* the wife
of Shallum the son of Tikvah, the son of Harhas,
keeper of the wardrobe; (now she dwelt in Jerusalem
in the college;) *and they communed with her.* And
she said unto them, Thus saith the LORD God of
Israel, *Tell the man that sent you to me,* Thus saith
the LORD, Behold, I will bring evil upon this place,
and upon the inhabitants thereof, even all the words
of the book which the king of Judah hath read:
Because they have forsaken me, and have burned
incense unto other gods, that they might provoke
me to anger with all the works of their hands; therefore my wrath shall be kindled against this place,
and shall not be quenched. *But to the king of Judah*
*which sent you to enquire of the* LORD, *thus shall ye*
*say to him, Thus saith the* LORD *God of Israel, As*
*touching the words which thou hast heard; Because*
*thine heart was tender, and thou hast humbled*
*thyself before the* LORD, *when thou heardest what I*
*spake against this place, and against the inhabitants*
*thereof, that they should become a desolation and a*
*curse, and hast rent thy clothes, and wept before me;*
*I also have heard thee, saith the* LORD. *Behold there-*
*fore, I will gather thee unto thy fathers, and thou*
*shalt be gathered into thy grave in peace; and thine*

*eyes shall not see all the evil which I will bring upon*
*this place. And they brought the king word again.*

—EMPHASIS ADDED_

Each time the Word was read to them, they repented
and changed their ways. The Lord had mandated the
prophet to write down the prophetic message they received,
and the children of Israel were also commanded to write
the commandment of the Lord on the breastplate of their
hearts and keep it before their eyes.

For instance, the Biblical prophets had secretaries
that recorded their declarations. Jeremiah had a scribe
that worked with him. When the prophetic messages
were destroyed by various authorities that detested some
of the prophetic utterances they heard, God instructed a
replacement.

> And it came to pass in the fourth year of Jehoiakim
> the son of Josiah king of Judah, that *this word came*
> *unto Jeremiah from the* LORD, *saying, Take thee a*
> *roll of a book, and write therein all the words that*
> *I have spoken unto thee against Israel,* and against
> Judah, and against all the nations, from the day I
> spake unto thee, from the days of Josiah, even unto
> this day. *It may be that the house of Judah will hear*
> *all the evil which I purpose to do unto them; that*
> *they may return every man from his evil way; that*
> *I may forgive their iniquity and their sin.* Then Jere-
> miah called Baruch the son of Neriah: and *Baruch*
> *wrote from the mouth of Jeremiah all the words of the*
> LORD, *which he had spoken unto him, upon a roll of*

*a book.* And Jeremiah commanded Baruch, saying, I am shut up; I cannot go into the house of the LORD: *Therefore go thou, and read in the roll, which thou hast written from my mouth, the words of the LORD in the ears of the people in the LORD's house upon the fasting day: and also thou shalt read them in the ears of all Judah that come out of their cities. It may be they will present their supplication before the LORD, and will return every one from his evil way:* for great is the anger and the fury that the LORD hath pronounced against this people.

And Baruch the son of Neriah did according to all that Jeremiah the prophet commanded him, reading in the book the words of the LORD in the LORD's house. And it came to pass in the fifth year of Jehoiakim the son of Josiah king of Judah, in the ninth month, that they proclaimed a fast before the LORD to all the people in Jerusalem, and to all the people that came from the cities of Judah unto Jerusalem. Then read Baruch in the book the words of Jeremiah in the house of the LORD, in the chamber of Gemariah the son of Shaphan the scribe, in the higher court, at the entry of the new gate of the LORD's house, in the ears of all the people. When Michaiah the son of Gemariah, the son of Shaphan, had heard out of the book all the words of the LORD, Then he went down into the king's house, into the scribe's chamber: and, lo, all the princes sat there, even Elishama the scribe, and Delaiah the son of Shemaiah, and Elnathan the son of Achbor, and Gemariah the son of Shaphan, and Zedekiah the son of Hananiah, and all the princes. *Then Michaiah declared unto them all the words that he had heard, when Baruch read the book in the ears of the people.* Therefore all the princes sent Jehudi the son of Nethaniah, the son of Shelemiah, the son of Cushi, unto Baruch, saying, Take in thine hand the roll wherein thou hast read in the ears of the people, and come. So Baruch the son of Neriah took the roll in his hand, and came unto them. And they said unto him, *Sit down now, and read it in our ears. So Baruch read it in their ears. Now it came to pass, when they had heard all the words, they were afraid both one and other, and said unto Baruch, We will surely tell the king of all these words. And they asked Baruch, saying, Tell us now, How didst thou write all these words at his mouth? Then Baruch answered them, He pronounced all these words unto me with his mouth, and I wrote them with ink in the book. Then said the princes unto Baruch, Go, hide thee, thou and Jeremiah; and let no man know where ye be.*

And they went in to the king into the court, but they laid up the roll in the chamber of Elishama the scribe, and told all the words in the ears of the king. So the king sent Jehudi to fetch the roll: and he took it out of Elishama the scribe's chamber. And Jehudi read it in the ears of the king, and in the ears of all the princes which stood beside the king. Now the king sat in the winterhouse in the ninth month: and there was a fire on the hearth burning before him. *And it came to pass, that when Jehudi had read three or four leaves, he cut it with the penknife, and cast it into the fire that was on the hearth, until all the roll was consumed in the fire that was on the hearth.*

*Yet they were not afraid, nor rent their garments, neither the king, nor any of his servants that heard all these words.* Nevertheless Elnathan and Delaiah and Gemariah had made intercession to the king that he would not burn the roll: but he would not hear them. But the king commanded Jerahmeel the son of Hammelech, and Seraiah the son of Azriel, and Shelemiah the son of Abdeel, to take Baruch the scribe and Jeremiah the prophet: *but the LORD hid them.*

Then the word of the LORD came to Jeremiah, after that the king had burned the roll, and the words which Baruch wrote at the mouth of Jeremiah, saying, *Take thee again another roll, and write in it all the former words that were in the first roll, which Jehoiakim the king of Judah hath burned.* And thou shalt say to Jehoiakim king of Judah, Thus saith the LORD; Thou hast burned this roll, saying, Why hast thou written therein, saying, The king of Babylon shall certainly come and destroy this land, and shall cause to cease from thence man and beast? Therefore thus saith the LORD of Jehoiakim king of Judah; He shall have none to sit upon the throne of David: and his dead body shall be cast out in the day to the heat, and in the night to the frost. And I will punish him and his seed and his servants for their iniquity; and I will bring upon them, and upon the inhabitants of Jerusalem, and upon the men of Judah, all the evil that I have pronounced against them; but they hearkened not. Then took Jeremiah another roll, and gave it to Baruch the scribe, the son of Neriah; who wrote therein from the mouth of

Jeremiah all the words of the book which Jehoiakim king of Judah had burned in the fire: and there were added besides unto them many like words.

—JEREMIAH 36:1–32, KJV,
EMPHASIS ADDED

Nobody's behavior, attitude, or reaction can change the written Word of God. Jeremiah's experience was not the first time God had reordered the replacement of the written Word when a scroll was destroyed. When Moses broke the tablets of the first Ten Commandments the Lord replaced them.

And it came to pass, as soon as he came nigh unto the camp, that he saw the calf, and the dancing: and Moses' anger waxed hot, *and he cast the tablets out of his hands, and brake them beneath the mount.*

…And the LORD said unto Moses, *Hew thee two tables of stone like unto the first: and I will write upon these tables the words that were in the first tables, which thou brakest.* And be ready in the morning, and come up in the morning unto mount Sinai, and present thyself there to me in the top of the mount. And no man shall come up with thee, neither let any man be seen throughout all the mount; neither let the flocks nor herds feed before that mount. And he hewed two tables of stone like unto the first; and Moses rose up early in the morning, and went up unto mount Sinai, as the LORD had commanded him, and took in his hand the two tables of stone.

—EXODUS 32:19; 34:1–4, KJV,
EMPHASIS ADDED

God replaced the written word so that the people will not be ignorant of His commandments.

> And you shall tell your son in that day, saying, "This is done because of what the LORD did for me when I came up from Egypt."
>
> —EXODUS 13:8

God also stated the reasons for the preservation of the written word thus:

> Let not mercy and truth forsake you; Bind them around your neck, Write them on the tablet of your heart.
>
> —PROVERBS 3:3

The spoken Word of God is written to serve as constant reminder:

> But the word is very near you, in your mouth and in your heart, that you may do it.
>
> —DEUTERONOMY 30:14

## The Negative Word

The negative words or statements that we hear in prophetic utterances are not evil oriented as humanly considered. Although a prophetic word may sound negative, because the human ear and mind are sensitive, we do not take time to examine the full context of the message, otherwise we will realize that the meaning or impact of the message is not evil oriented.

The prophetic word is a progressive language that calls the attention of people to what God requires from them. When the language is heavy and burdensome, the people are expected to go before the Lord and repent. Some prophetic messages are negative because God expects us to change our ways. Ministers and leaders must not repel a prophet because the word for a particular season sounds negative.

In 1996, I went to minister in a church in Europe. During the ministration I had a prophetic word for the church. The prophetic word revealed that there were rebels in the church and the Lord was giving them a note of warning to repent. Both the pastor and the leaders were offended. In fact, the pastor took over the pulpit. Instead of calling for repentance, he began to defend his congregation members against the prophetic word that was spoken.

As the pastor defended his church members, I heard the Lord said, "This pastor is trying to play god over deception. His ministry is going to suffer from the hands of the rebels who have planned to throw him out." The Lord also said to me, "I would have exposed the rebels if he had respected your ministry and called for repentance."

A few months later, the prophetic word came to pass. One of the assistant ministers and some leaders took over the church and threw him out. The pastor quickly salvaged himself by going off to rent a new place for church services within the week of the commotion, in an attempt to gain the following of the majority. Yet a few went with him to the new church. For years, he struggled to build up the new place.

Although the prophetic word was negative, it was meant to salvage his ministry, not to destroy him. When a prophetic word for a season sounds negative, it is time to fast and pray for mercy. The ministers are supposed to lead the people in the prayer of repentance and perpetual change of heart. The Scripture says:

> If my people who are called by My name will humble themselves, and pray and seek My face, and turn from their wicked ways, then I will hear from heaven, and will forgive their sin and heal their land. Now My eyes will be open and My ears attentive to prayer made in this place.
>
> —2 CHRONICLES 7:14–15

Some of the words or language that the human mind refuses to hear in prophecy include: judgment, condemnation, and warning.

**Warning**

Prophetic warning is the process of releasing information that reveals a danger. It is a cautionary notice of mishap. God warns us when the enemy is planning to invade our peace. He also warns us when we are about to go wrong. When we misbehave or transgress His laws, He sends us a prophetic word that exposes our sins and propels us to repent and change our ways.

Prophetic warning precedes judgment. Warning comes before judgment is considered. Warning is the caution that God gives to people through the prophets. The sound of warning comes when a person or a people are living in sin. The prophetic warning is given to make people aware that they are going astray and far away from God.

If the people do not yield to the warning, then God will release the prophetic judgment. If the people do not heed the warning, then the situation may attract condemnation, because the people are stiff-necked.

Jeremiah was a prophet of warning and judgment. He gave the warning but the people did not receive the word. The prophetic message moved on to relay the dissatisfaction of the Lord—the impending judgment that awaited disobedience.

The individuals that repented were spared from condemnation, while some ignorant persons were affected. The stubborn ones suffered from the hook of slavery along with the disobedient king Jeconiah. Those who repented later were released to return to Israel.

Prophetic warnings include: impending evil, progressive evil, and war of the season.

*Impending evil*

God warns His people through the prophet when there is an impending evil. Hosea and Amos were prophets who played a cautionary role in the life of Israel. Their messages were prophetic warnings to Israel. Hosea referred to Israel as "harlots."

> Though thou, *Israel, play the harlot,* yet let not Judah offend; and come not ye unto Gilgal, neither go ye up to Bethaven, nor swear, The LORD liveth.
>
> —HOSEA 4:15, KJV,
> EMPHASIS ADDED

Amos described them as "cows of Bashan."

> *Hear this word, ye kine of Bashan,* that are in the mountain of Samaria, which oppress the poor, which crush the needy, which say to their masters, Bring, and let us drink. The Lord GOD hath sworn by his holiness, that, lo, the days shall come upon you, that he will take you away with hooks, and your posterity with fishhooks. And ye shall go out at the breaches, every cow at that which is before her; and ye shall cast them into the palace, saith the LORD. Come to Bethel, and transgress; at Gilgal multiply transgression; and bring your sacrifices every morning, and your tithes after three years.
>
> —AMOS 4:1–4, KJV,
> EMPHASIS ADDED

### Progressive evil

The prophetic warning continues as long as the people progress in their evil way. When evil exceeds righteousness, the prophetic warning progresses. Noah gave the people a progressive warning for over four hundred years before the flood came as judgment and condemnation. Progressive evil means being stiff-necked, stubbornness, rebellion, disobedience, and spiritual wickedness in high places.

*War of the season*

The prophetic message is to create an awareness of the season in which we live. Sometimes people are not conscious of the wiles of the enemy and the warfare in the spiritual realms. Hezekiah was not conscious of the battle in the realms of the spirit when he invited a Babylonian envoy into his palace. Ignorantly he showed them the secret of his wealth and all that was in the house of the Lord. Following that invitation, the Babylonians became envious and began to harass Hezekiah the king of Judah.

> And Isaiah said, This sign shalt thou have of the LORD, that the LORD will do the thing that he hath spoken: shall the shadow go forward ten degrees, or go back ten degrees? And Hezekiah answered, It is a light thing for the shadow to go down ten degrees: nay, but let the shadow return backward ten degrees. And Isaiah the prophet cried unto the LORD: and he brought the shadow ten degrees backward, by which it had gone down in the dial of Ahaz.
>
> At that time Berodachbaladan, the son of Baladan, king of Babylon, sent letters and a present unto Hezekiah: for he had heard that Hezekiah had been sick. And Hezekiah hearkened unto them, and shewed them all the house of his precious things, the silver, and the gold, and the spices, and the precious ointment, and all the house of his armour, and all that was found in his treasures: there was nothing in his house, nor in all his dominion, that Hezekiah shewed them not. Then came Isaiah the prophet unto king Hezekiah, and said unto him, What

said these men? and from whence came they unto thee? And Hezekiah said, *They are come from a far country, even from Babylon. And he said, What have they seen in thine house? And Hezekiah answered, All the things that are in mine house have they seen: there is nothing among my treasures that I have not shewed them. And Isaiah said unto Hezekiah, Hear the word of the* Lord. *Behold, the days come, that all that is in thine house, and that which thy fathers have laid up in store unto this day, shall be carried into Babylon: nothing shall be left, saith the* Lord.

—2 Kings 20:9–19, kjv,
EMPHASIS ADDED

## Judgment

Judgment points out the good or evil that concerns a matter. The word judgment is not an evil word and it is not the final product of a case. Judgment is the process of finding out the truth of a matter, and deciphering between the good or evil involved in it. Judgment is the summation of a matter that is causing fury between two parties or individuals.

In a prophetic message, the usage of the term judgment is a presentation of the summary of human behavior, which could either be pleasing or unpleasing to God. Whenever the term judgment is used in a prophecy, it means God is demanding repentance and reconciliation from the person or people concerned. Therefore prophetic judgment is the method by which God attracts repentance, forgiveness, and reconciliation from his people.

## Condemnation

Condemnation is the conviction that is laid upon a person or a people after a matter has been judged and the findings are concluded. When repentance and reconciliation fail after a judgment has been passed, then condemnation is applied. Jesus came not to condemn the world, but that through repentance and remission of sin, people would receive pardon and be reconciled unto God.

*For God sent not his Son into the world to condemn the world; but that the world through him might be saved.* He that believeth on him is not condemned: but he that believeth not is condemned already, because he hath not believed in the name of the only begotten Son of God. *And this is the condemnation,* that light is come into the world, and *men loved darkness rather than light,* because their deeds were evil. For every one that doeth evil hateth the light, neither cometh to the light, lest his deeds should be reproved.

—JOHN 3:17–20, KJV,
EMPHASIS ADDDED

Condemnation is the repercussion or the consequences of the judgment if one refuses to yield to repentance. Condemnation is the punishment that follows conviction after a matter has been judged. Repentance can turn a judgment of condemnation around and release pardon unto a person. Barabbas was condemned to death. He was later on released and Jesus Christ died in place of him. Jesus died that he might be free; and today, we have received the freedom from our condemnation of sin because we confess Jesus as Lord and Savior. The prophetic word reprimands us to change our ways so that we will not perish but have everlasting life. Amen!

# Chapter 8

# UNDERSTANDING AND INTERPRETATION

P ROPHETIC INTERPRETATION IS probably the most interesting aspect of the prophetic ministry. Prophetic interpretation is related to the prophetic language. It is another realm of prophetic utterance. The prophetic language is quite unique. It is simple but very deep. When Joseph stood before Pharaoh to interpret the dream that had troubled the king's mind, little did he know that he was about to step into his destiny. Although it seems that he was interpreting Pharaoh's dream, he was actually prophesying his own destiny into existence. Pharaoh's dream was a propellant to Joseph's destiny. Joseph's prophetic interpretation was also a promotion from prison to the position of a prime minister in a foreign land.

> And Joseph said unto Pharaoh, The dream of Pharaoh is one: *God hath shewed Pharaoh what he is about to do*....And for that the dream was doubled unto Pharaoh twice; it is because the thing is established by God, and God will shortly bring it to pass. *Now therefore let Pharaoh look out a man discreet and wise, and set him over the land of Egypt.* Let Pharaoh do this, and let him appoint officers over the land, and take up the fifth part of the land of Egypt in the seven plenteous years. And let them gather all the food of those good years that come, and lay up corn under the hand of Pharaoh, and let them keep food in the cities. And that food shall be for store to the land against the seven years of famine, which shall be in the land of Egypt; that the land perish not through the famine. *And the thing was good in the eyes of Pharaoh, and in the eyes of all his servants.* And Pharaoh said unto his servants, *Can we find such a one as this is, a man in whom the Spirit of God is?* And Pharaoh said unto Joseph, *Forasmuch as God hath shewed thee all this; there is none so discreet and wise as thou art:* Thou shalt be over my house, and *according unto thy word shall all my people be ruled: only in the throne will I be greater than thou.* And Pharaoh said unto Joseph, See, I have set thee over all the land of Egypt. *And Pharaoh took off his ring from his hand, and put it upon Joseph's hand, and arrayed him in vestures of fine linen, and put a gold chain about his neck;* And

he made him to ride in the second chariot which he had; and *they cried before him, Bow the knee: and he made him ruler over all the land of Egypt.* And Pharaoh said unto Joseph, I am Pharaoh, and without thee shall no man lift up his hand or foot in all the land of Egypt....And *Joseph was thirty years old when he stood before Pharaoh king of Egypt.* And Joseph went out from the presence of Pharaoh, and went throughout all the land of Egypt. And in the seven plenteous years the earth brought forth by handfuls. And he gathered up all the food of the seven years, which were in the land of Egypt, and laid up the food in the cities: the food of the field, which was round about every city, laid he up in the same. And Joseph gathered corn as the sand of the sea, very much, until he left numbering; for it was without number....And when all the land of Egypt was famished, the people cried to Pharaoh for bread: and Pharaoh said unto all the Egyptians, *Go unto Joseph; what he saith to you, do.* And the famine was over all the face of the earth: And Joseph opened all the storehouses, and sold unto the Egyptians; and the famine waxed sore in the land of Egypt. *And all countries came into Egypt to Joseph for to buy corn*; because that the famine was so sore in all lands.

—GENESIS 41:25, 32–44, 46–49, 55–57, KJV,
EMPHASIS ADDED

## What Is Prophetic Interpretation?

Prophetic interpretation is a type of wisdom that unravels a prodigy or a mystery. It is a power that opens up the secret behind a phenomenon.

Prophetic interpretation is the act of explaining the meaning of a parable, an omen, or a matter that is connected to the spirit realm. It is the ability to understand spiritual things in simple terms. It is a skill that explicates matters of different realms and puts them in functional places in the physical realm.

Also, prophetic interpretation is a type of prophetic insight that opens up the eyes of the prophet, to perceive the totality of a revelation and explain it as though he or she has been involved in the reality of that revelation. Prophetic interpretation enables a prophet to present a message with a graphic expression as though he or she has a prior knowledge of the situation.

Prophetic interpretation brings forth the wholeness of a revelation in its progressive form, thus, relaying and coordinating the past with the present and the future manifestation of that which has been revealed.

For instance, Joseph was able to relay Pharaoh's dream—by revealing the depth of the message from the present into the far future. Joseph was also able to co-ordinate the meaning of the revelation in reality as he supervised the years of plenty and the years of famine in Egypt.

# What Is Prophetic Understanding?

Prophetic understanding is a unique ability to comprehend the meaning of an omen with simplicity. It is an ability to grasp the significance or importance of information conveyed or portrayed in a revelation. It means to have a systematic interpretation and explanation of the rational behind a revelation or an omen.

Prophetic understanding is a superior power of discerning spiritual things. It is the demonstration of spiritual intelligence by elucidating a spiritual message. Scripture states that God gave Daniel and his associates knowledge and skill in all literature and wisdom. This unique competence enabled Daniel and his friends to have understanding in all visions and dreams. In view of this prowess, Daniel and his acquaintances were able to interpret all matters of wisdom and understanding that were presented to them. By the act of wisdom, these gentlemen avoided compromise and indulgence in activities that would contaminate their faith in God.

Consequently, Daniel and his companions were found ten times better than all the magicians and astrologers who were in all the realms of Babylon. Daniel's unique understanding of things that pertain to the realms of the spirit and the physical enabled him to expose the source of King Nebuchadnezzar's dream and vision, as well as their contents.

Before revealing the secrets of king Nebuchadnezzar's dreams and visions, Daniel demonstrated an act of wisdom when he cautioned the motive that influenced the revelation by stating thus: "that you may know the thoughts of your heart" (Dan. 2:30).

> Daniel answered in the presence of the king, and said, The secret which the king hath demanded cannot the wise men, the astrologers, the magicians, the soothsayers, shew unto the king; *But there is a God in heaven that revealeth secrets*, and maketh known to the king Nebuchadnezzar what shall be in the latter days. *Thy dream, and the visions of thy head upon thy bed, are these*; As for thee, O king, *thy thoughts came into thy mind upon thy bed*, what should come to pass hereafter: and *he that revealeth secrets maketh known to thee what shall come to pass*. But as for me, this secret is not revealed to me for any wisdom that I have more than any living, but for their sakes that shall make known the interpretation to the king, *and that thou mightest know the thoughts of thy heart.*
>
> —DANIEL 2:27–30, KJV,
> EMPHASIS ADDED

Following the caution, Daniel moved on to narrate the king's dream and visions as though he had witnessed the scenario in real life (Dan. 2:31–35). After the narration, Daniel then presented the interpretation in this manner: "This is the dream. Now we will tell the interpretation of it before the king" (v. 36).

Daniel was a man of excellent wisdom and understanding. He demonstrated his prowess by distinguishing the revelation from the interpretation. As much as God revealed the details of every secret and the motive that influenced the dream as being the thoughts of the king's head, Daniel did not muzzle the presentation. He did not interfere with the interpretation as he explained it in simple meaning to the king. The king identified with Daniel's interpretation and also recognized the Spirit of God in Daniel.

> The king answered unto Daniel, and said, *Of a truth it is, that your God is a God of gods, and a Lord of kings, and a revealer of secrets,* seeing thou couldest reveal this secret. Then the king made Daniel a great man, and gave him many great gifts, and made him ruler over the whole province of Babylon, and chief of the governors over all the wise men of Babylon.
> —DANIEL 2:47–48, KJV,
> EMPHASIS ADDED

People who exercise the gift of prophecy, the word of knowledge, the word of wisdom and discernment of spirits and other revelatory gifts, must learn to decipher between what is the actual revelation and what is the interpretation, as well as their personal understanding or assumption. Daniel applied wisdom to the presentation of the revelation and its interpretation to the king. Although the meaning of the dream was harsh, the king did not blame Daniel but received it with gratitude and promoted Daniel and his companions.

# Interpreting the Prophetic Language

## Times and seasons

After the flood that destroyed the earth, Noah offered thanksgiving offerings to God. The Lord smelled the aroma of Noah's offering and promised in His heart, never to destroy every living thing as He had done. As part of the covenant, the Lord used the significance of season and time to establish the manifestation of His promises to humans thus.

> And Noah builded an altar unto the LORD; and took of every clean beast, and of every clean fowl, and offered burnt offerings on the altar. And the LORD smelled a sweet savour; and the LORD said in his heart, I will not again curse the ground any more for man's sake; for the imagination of man's heart *is* evil from his youth; neither will I again smite any more every thing living, as I have done. While the earth remaineth, *seedtime and harvest, and cold and heat, and summer and winter, and day and night shall not cease.*
>
> —GENESIS 8:20–22, KJV,
> EMPHASIS ADDED

This passage of Scripture reveals that the Lord has made a declaration to relate to His creatures with the act of season and time factor. Seeds are planted at a particular seasons of the year. Besides a specified season, the seeds are also sowed at a particular time of the day. Similarly, the fruits that spring up from the seeds that were planted are also harvested at a particular period of the year. Also, for the purpose of preservation of quality and freshness, some products are harvested at a particular time of the day.

In view of this divine declaration, farmers are conscious of the seasons of sowing and harvesting their crops. Both natural, or organic, and scientific farmers are very conscious of the time and season for planting and harvesting; otherwise, certain birds and pests will interfere with their products while the challenges of the weather will also affect the quality and quantity of production.

God has deliberately created a strategy for planting seeds and harvesting of fruits and crops. This process of farming is strongly applicable to the prophetic word and interpretation of divine oracle.

### God's plans and purposes

The plans and purposes of God are scheduled to manifest according to a specific season and time. That is why the sun rises in the morning and goes down in the evening. Except by the act of divine intervention and manifestation, the clock never goes backward, but always moves forward.

Ecclesiastes 3:1-15 (KJV) also talks about the importance of season and time construct.

> *To every thing there is a season, and a time to every*
> *purpose under the heaven: A time to be born, and*
> *a time to die; a time to plant, and a time to pluck*
> *up that which is planted; A time to kill, and a time*

to heal; a time to break down, and a time to build up; A time to weep, and a time to laugh; a time to mourn, and a time to dance; A time to cast away stones, and a time to gather stones together; a time to embrace, and a time to refrain from embracing; A time to get, and a time to lose; a time to keep, and a time to cast away; A time to rend, and a time to sew; a time to keep silence, and a time to speak; A time to love, and a time to hate; a time of war, and a time of peace. What profit hath he that worketh in that wherein he laboureth? *I have seen the travail, which God hath given to the sons of men to be exercised in it. He hath made every thing beautiful in his time: also he hath set the world in their heart,* so that no man can find out the work that God maketh from the beginning to the end.

I know that there is no good in them, but for a man to rejoice, and to do good in his life. And also that every man should eat and drink, and enjoy the good of all his labour, it is the gift of God. I know that, whatsoever God doeth, it shall be for ever: nothing can be put to it, nor any thing taken from it: and God doeth it, that men should fear before him. That which hath been is now; and that which is to be hath already been; and God requireth that which is past.

—EMPHASIS ADDED

No matter the number of prophecies uttered over a person and the length of prophecies that have been given, one still has to wait for the time of reaping to harvest the fruits or crops according to the seasons scheduled for them.

Even if a seed is fertilized and induced for quick production, there will always be a time factor connected to the principles of sowing and reaping. No prophet can change the plans and purposes of God. However, if a prophet acts in time and season, things will definitely fall in place as scheduled by divine order.

Sometimes a prophet may speak over a person in a season that is already ripe, so that prophetic word would produce instant manifestation in the realm of harvest. Hence, the word that is spoken would come to pass within that season because the seed that has been sown was set for harvest.

**The prophetic harvesters**

There are prophets who are called to release people into their season of harvest. From my observation of this realm of function, I will describe such persons as prophetic harvesters. Thus the prophetic harvesters are sharp and can easily sense things that are happening in a person's life from the spiritual realm. They are able to discern the arrangements of events that have been laid down for a particular era. Such prophets normally make utterances with specific mention of date and time and also give signals that indicate a time of manifestation of an oracle.

The prophetic harvester propels a person to step into a specific destination connected to the manifestation of a particular event. The prophetic harvester can only present that which God has already destined for a person or a situation. He or she cannot change or alter God's word.

However, a prophet can supplicate for divine intervention in a matter that is not originally God's will but was fostered by the act of disobedience. For instance, Abraham supplicated for Sodom in a matter that was not God's will to destroy. Thus, considering the covenant that God made with Noah after the flood, it was not God's will to destroy the people and the city of Sodom and Gomorrah. Hence, for the sake of the righteous, God spared the life of Lot and some members of his family (Gen. 18:16–33). Also, Moses supplicated for the children of Israel by referring God to the promises He had made to Abraham, Isaac, and Jacob. God listened to Moses and relented from destroying the children of Israel in the wilderness, because it was not part of His original plans to erase them from the earth, but to take them to the promise land.

## Time

Time formulates the operations of a season. It is an element that operates within a season. It is the component that counts the segment of a season.

Time reveals the progression of a season. It is the proponent of periods that constitute the allocation of moments in seconds, minutes, and hours that result in the measuring of day and night.

Time is the portion of an event that constitutes a season. It expresses the duration of an event. It indicates an interval for specific occasion. It reveals the accuracy and promptness that is given to the response of a situation or phenomenon.

More often than not, the prophetic word is strongly related to time. Time plays an important role in prophecy. Like the conception of a pregnancy, the prophetic word is generated by time construct. Thus like a seed, one is supposed to take note of the time and season that the prophetic word is released. Also it is pertinent to watch over the maturation of the word that has been spoken. There is also a need to be alert and careful not to abort the manifestation of the word or kill the process of delivery when birth pains begin. Many people want babies, but they cannot endure the labor pain; so also, many people want the prophetic word, but they cannot tolerate the process of maturity and gestation that leads to fulfillment.

It is important that time is respected in the realm of the prophetic word that is released to us. People operating in the prophetic office must be conscious of the role that time plays in the delivery of a message. Time may affect a message positively or negatively depending on the circumstances surrounding the content of the message. Recipients of the prophetic word must also take not of the time that the message comes to them. Time plays an active role in the development and fulfillment of the prophetic word.

**Seasons**

Season is a flavor that attracts the manifestation of spiritual things. When a tree is matured for production, the spirit of productivity will connect with the flavor of the season, and there will be a magnetic pollination for fertilization that will influence the production of the fruits for that period.

The prophetic word moves with season. Prophetic season is the time that God has purposed for something to manifest either systematically or promptly. Prophetic season may be revealed in part before it enters into complete manifestation and fulfillment.

Prophetic manifestation and fulfillment take place in specific seasons that have been allocated according to the plans and purposes of God the Creator. Like a mango or orange tree that bears fruit in a specific time of the year, the prophetic word is released to operate in a unique manner that fashions the purpose for which it is sent forth.

For instance, if the prophetic word is sent forth as a seed into the life of a person, then that seed may need to be nurtured in order to germinate in the life of the person. It may also need some of attention or care to grow up to fulfill its purpose. The prophetic word that is a seed needs to become a tree in order for it to bear fruit in the season allotted to it.

A prophetic word that is released in the form of a seed will need to be properly nurtured with fertilizer, which is prayer, fasting, and study of the Scripture in preparation for fruitfulness. Otherwise that seed will struggle to survive and it may be delayed because it is not properly fostered.

Sometimes the prophetic word is released in the form of an egg or a yolk which both represent pregnancy. And sometimes the word comes forth directly as a pregnancy depending on the level of understanding and preparation for the purpose of the revelation. Sometimes one is very close to delivery or birthing a destiny as of the time that one is receiving the prophetic word.

Therefore the conception can be either close to maturity or birthing. When a pregnancy is close to maturity, the recipient has to prepare for laboring. That is why it is dangerous for people to go about collecting prophecies instead of studying the Word of God to groom themselves in preparation for birthing a destiny.

Some Christian brothers and sisters are like pregnant people who do not know how to take care of their pregnancies. Instead of sticking to one medical center and medical personnel, they go all over the place seeking people to father their pregnancies and also seeking the opinion of all kinds of medical personnel to confirm their pregnancies and the gender of the babies in their wombs.

In the process, the babies are messed up by the dangerous prescriptions that emerge from parental or medical carelessness. Hence, there are many people who have received hundreds of prophecies, yet they are confused and frustrated because nothing seems to be happening. The problem is that this category of individuals has not learned to discipline themselves for discipleship. Some of them are not submissive to authority because of the prophecies they have received. The truth is that these individuals who are prophecy conscious do not know how to work out their salvation. They are hungry and thirsty for home cooked food, but they are yet to identify their personal needs. Rather, they go about nibbling on snacks that have no balanced diet and feeding on fast food that has no nutritional sustenance.

### A word in season

A word in season is a ministration that takes place when it is rightly required to satisfy a need in time. Sometimes a prophetic word in season comes to us through individuals and circumstances that are connected to our destinies. Some acts are divinely linked up to the fulfillment of our destinies. Such actions or moves that are divinely connected to the fulfillment of our destinies will be manifested either through a prophetic utterance, prophetic revelation, or a prophetic move or action. Acts such as marriage, childbearing, involvement in ministry, and church activities, as well as obedience to instructions, are propellants to prophetic manifestations. Some of these moves easily lead to manifestation of God's design for one's destiny.

For instance, women usually have a season of attraction for love and marriage. During the season of attraction, a lady becomes like a variety of ripe fruit on a mango or orange tree. Men who are attracted by certain types of mangoes or oranges are drawn to propose marriage to a "ripe mango or orange lady." A lady who is sensitive to her season of marriage responds with wisdom, while a lady who is ignorant of her season may ignore the winking eyes connected to her season.

If a ripe mango or orange lady walks into an environment where there is a person or minister who is prophetic or spiritually sensitive, someone will see a revelation that signifies marriage for the ripe fruit lady.

One Sunday afternoon in 1995 after ministering in a church in East London, we were waiting for a ride when I noticed one of the ladies from the church. She was glittering like a pearl. As she drew closer to us, I started smelling the fragrance of a mango. Then I turned to the pastor and asked if this lady was married or in a relationship? The pastor decided to call her instead of answering my question. So I posed the question again in the presence of the pastor. Then the pastor asked, "Why?" Then I said, "She is beaming like a ripe mango ready for marriage." They all burst into laughter and for some minutes, the lady was giggling.

The lady was very excited because she had been struggling with a decision as to whether the proposal she had received was from the Lord or not. In fact, she was supposed to give a gentleman a response that afternoon. That was an answered prayer for her. She later told her pastor that the statement I made helped her decision. Indeed, she was a mango ripe lady ready for the altar to say "I do."

On another occasion, I saw a lady who was ripe in her season but differently. Instead of smelling the mangoes and the oranges, I was hearing the sound of a bridal march. When I looked at her, I saw her wearing a beautiful wedding gown decorated with pearls. For several months I saw her in pearls.

Then suddenly the fragrance of a variety of fruits followed. One day I was led to give her a word that her husband was abroad and that she should get ready to travel. She did not receive it. At another time, I was led to tell her to get ready for marriage. She became upset and started to avoid me.

A few months later, the pastor announced her wedding that was to take place in another part of the world. Hence, she would be departing the country as soon as her visa was ready. Wow! Everybody turned their eyes on me and smiled. After the service, several ladies who had heard that I gave her the word came to me and narrated how she had disliked me for telling her about marriage. And now she was traveling abroad for the wedding ceremony.

Many people are too "righteous" to pay attention to their season of manifestation and fulfillment. We need to be conscious and sensitive to times and seasons connected to the prophetic message that fulfills our destiny.

**A word out of season**

A word out of season is when a message is delivered to a person at a time that one does not understand or have a clue what it is all about. It is also when a person is given a word at a time that a person is not ready for it. The person may reject the word or receive it depending on his or her understanding of prophecies.

However, it is important that prayer and intercession be made to preserve a prophetic message, even if the word is not properly presented to us. Do not repel a prophetic utterance even if it sounds foolish or inadequate. Like a treasure, store it in the bank of life or in a storage place—

like a diary—and watch and pray over it. One day you will find that word useful and important for restoration.

A word out of season is not false or useless. It is just a word that is given earlier than scheduled or at a time when the recipient is ignorant or not ready for such a message. When the time ripens, the word will be required to meet special needs.

- Season is a creative word for time construct or construction of time.

- Season has no limitation.

- Season has ability to fertilize amidst reception.

- Time is a specific construct.

- Time is limited.

- Time construct affects prophetic utterances positively or negatively.

## Why Do Prophecies Tarry?

There are several reasons that may affect the manifestation and fulfillment of prophecies. Some prophecies are fulfilled unnoticed, some are delayed, and others are transferred to some other persons or nations. Usually prophecies are delayed or transferred to other persons or organizations or nations because of the act of disobedience.

When our behaviors and attitudes refuse correction and pruning, we are likely to suffer prophetic delay or transfer. For instance, the parents of the Exodus who left Egypt did not see the Promised Land because of disobedient, stubborn, and rebellious behaviors. The inheritances of parents were transferred to the children.

Some of the reasons that affect the fulfillment of prophecies are: insensitivity, sluggishness, disobedience, stubbornness, and complacency.

## Insensitivity

Prophecy may tarry when a person is not sensitive to time and season. For instance, many gracious and active church ladies have lost their time and season for marriage because they were not sensitive to their age.

Insensitivity may cause a delay or denial in the manifestation of prophecies because the person or people involved are not listening or attentive. They are praying, but they are not watching the times and the seasons. The denial here means that some of the people involved may never witness the manifestation of the prophecy because they are not sensitive. The prophecy is likely to be fulfilled after they have departed this earth and gone to glory.

## Sluggishness

A person who is not smart may miss the timing of a prophetic manifestation that is connected to a specific time of the day, walking or moving to a place, or responding to a call or assignment.

Sluggishness is a type of laziness. People who are sluggish or too slow may miss a prophetic timing and season. Hence, there will be a delay in responding to manifestations. In the process, the manifestation will be enjoyed by other persons who did not actually receive the prophecy. Ecclesiastes 10:18 (KJV) says, "By much slothfulness the building decayeth; and through idleness of the hands the house droppeth through."

## Disobedience

A person who is not prone to responding to authority may unconsciously repel a prophetic voice that is meant to birth the manifestation of a particular word into reality. For instance, forty days became forty years of journey from Egypt to the Promised Land because of disobedience. Israel was delayed in the wilderness because some of them rebelled against the authority of Moses.

Disobedience may cause a delay in manifestation of prophecies or transfer to another person who is submissive.

## Stubbornness

A person who is stubborn may unconsciously opposed a prophetic move. By so doing, he or she may never be fulfilled because opposition breeds rebellion and rejection of truth. For instance, rebellion and stubbornness can cause a switch of anointing from one person to another, as Saul's kingly anointing was transferred to David.

Stubbornness may cause a prophecy and anointing to be transferred to another person either within the family or outside of the family. Sometimes a friend or an active member of the ministry may inherit the call, blessing, or promise.

**Complacency**

People who do not consider the need to work out his or her salvation may be expecting God to do everything for them automatically. Hence, little or no effort is made to prepare oneself for the manifestation and fulfillment of the prophetic message that has been received.

Complacency may cause a delay or denial in the manifestation of a prophecy. The denial means that the prophecy will likely be manifested or fulfilled unnoticed, because the individuals or persons concerned are lazy or are not alert or smart.

# Prophetic Signs and Symbols

Daniel's prophetic messages were received in:

- Visions and dreams

Ezekiel's prophecies were received and demonstrated in:

- Parables
- Metaphors
- Signs
- Symbols

# Prophetic Symbols

Geographical features, resources, and climate have a strong relationship with the prophetic language and interpretation. Also weather is a condition of nature that usually constitutes prophetic language and symbols. Therefore, in order to understand prophetic symbols, one has to understand the language of nature.

Prophetic symbols are related to the supernatural work of God and the natural things that surround human existence. God uses the work of His hands to speak to us. (See Isaiah 45:11.)

The works of God's hands are the supernatural things that formulate the natural. The things that have been given to mankind on earth are natural, and the things that pertain to the spiritual realm (the throne of God) are supernatural. Humans were created by God (supernatural) to live on the earth (natural). Similarly, there is a characteristic that is unnatural because it came with the fall of mankind in the Garden of Eden. God created the good but permitted evil because of the sin of disobedience. (See Genesis 2:16–17.)

## The Waters

*Waters* is a word that represents different types of natural liquid that cover the structure of the earth. Waters are identified by names according to their divisions and constitutions in the geographical structure of the earth. Waters form the composition of the sea or ocean, rivers, lakes, lagoon, streams, and waterfalls. The earth and everything in it was formed out of the waters.

> In the beginning God created the heaven and the earth. And the earth was without form, and void;

and darkness was upon the face of the deep. And *the Spirit of God moved upon the face of the waters.* And God said, Let there be light: and there was light. And God saw the light, that it was good: and God divided the light from the darkness. And God called the light Day, and the darkness he called Night. And the evening and the morning were the first day.

And God said, *Let there be a firmament in the midst of the waters, and let it divide the waters from the waters. And God* made the firmament, and *divided the waters which were under the firmament from the waters which were above the firmament:* and it was so. And God called the firmament Heaven. And the evening and the morning were the second day.

And God said, *Let the waters under the heaven be gathered together unto one place,* and let the dry land appear: and it was so. And God called the dry land Earth; and *the gathering together of the waters called he Seas:* and God saw that it was good.

—GENESIS 1:1–10, KJV,
EMPHASIS ADDED

## Water

Water has a great impact in the prophetic language. Water has so many interpretations. The interpretation of water in a particular revelation depends on the situation and circumstances surrounding it. All situations that involve water do not mean the same.

Under the term water, we have the following:

- A symbol of the Holy Spirit

*Fountain*

Fountain of water is a symbol of wisdom, abundance, and joy of life.

> Israel then shall dwell in safety alone: the fountain of Jacob shall be upon a land of corn and wine; also his heavens shall drop down dew.
>
> —DEUTERONOMY 33: 28, KJV

Fountain is also a symbol of forgiveness, cleansing and healing.

> In that day *there shall be a fountain opened to the house of David* and to the inhabitants of Jerusalem *for sin and for uncleanness.* And it shall come to pass in that day, saith the LORD of hosts, that I will cut off the names of the idols out of the land, and they shall no more be remembered: and also *I will cause the prophets and the unclean spirit to pass out of the land.*
>
> —ZECHARIAH 13:1–2, KJV

## Spring

Spring of water is a symbol of life, peace, knowledge, wisdom, understanding, treasure, wealth, and abundance.

> For the LORD thy God bringeth thee into a good land, a land of brooks of water, of fountains and depths that spring out of valleys and hills.
>
> —DEUTERONOMY 8:7, KJV

### Gushing water

It means repentance, forgiveness, and healing.

### Stagnant water

Still water may be good or bad depending on the atmosphere of the revelation. It either means the peace of God or a dumping ground—a lagoon.

A lagoon is a dumping ground. It is an artificial pool where dirty water from a septic tank, drainage, or sewer system is discarded. Usually a lagoon stinks.

### Rivers

Rivers of living water:

> He that believeth on me, as the scripture hath said, out of his belly shall flow rivers of living water.
> —JOHN 7:38, KJV

A river is a symbol of long life, treasure, natural resources, unique abilities, and wisdom. It also refers to a supernatural endowment and divine impartation from the Most High. A river may be rich in natural resources such gold, silver, and other precious stones. A river may also be rich in living things like fish. Some rivers are full of abundance of wealth.

> And *a river went out of Eden to water the garden*; and from thence it was parted, and became into four heads. The name of the *first is Pison*: that is it which compasseth the whole land of Havilah, *where*

*there is gold And the gold of that land is good: there is bdellium and the onyx stone.*

And the name of the *second river is Gihon*: the same is it that compasseth the whole land of Ethiopia. And the name of *the third river is Hiddekel*: that is it which goeth toward the east of Assyria. And *the fourth river is Euphrates. And the* LORD *God took the man, and put him into the garden of Eden to dress it and to keep it.*

—GENESIS 2:10–15, KJV,
EMPHASIS ADDED

## Flood

A flood is a good and bad omen. The interpretation of a particular revelation that is connected to a flood must be narrated in full in order for one to understand the message involved.

A flood may represent abundance or overflow of blessings. Where there has been some type of lack, poverty, or drought, a revelation of a flood will mean healing, restoration, and abundance of blessings.

In another event a flood may symbolize judgment or destruction depending on the circumstances of the revelation. The Lord destroyed the earth with a flood of water from rainfall during Noah's age. Noah and his family were protected in the great ark during the flood of destruction.

## Rain

Rainfall means abundance—an outpouring of God's presence and blessings. It also means restoration and new beginnings—the later rain and the former rain. Rainfall also represents healing and cleansing.

> But the land, whither ye go to possess it, is a land of hills and valleys, and *drinketh water of the rain of heaven*: A land which the LORD thy God careth for: *the eyes of the LORD thy God are always upon it*, from the beginning of the year even unto the end of the year. And it shall come to pass, if ye shall hearken diligently unto my commandments which I command you this day, to love the LORD your God, and to serve him with all your heart and with all your soul, That *I will give you the rain of your land in his due season, the first rain and the latter rain, that thou mayest gather in thy corn, and thy wine, and thine oil,* And I will send grass in thy fields for thy cattle, that thou mayest eat and be full.
>
> —DEUTERONOMY 11:11–15, KJV,
> EMPHASIS ADDED

> The LORD shall open unto thee his good treasure, *the heaven to give the rain unto thy land in his season*, and to bless all the work of thine hand: and thou shalt lend unto many nations, and thou shalt not borrow.
>
> —DEUTERONOMY 28:12, KJV,
> EMPHASIS ADDED

### Dew of heaven

The dew is a glistening moisture that nature showers into the atmosphere to wet the earth. The dew is a phenomenon that symbolizes the release of blessings from heaven.

The dew was used as a term to indicate the manifestation of the Abrahamic covenant blessings with his descendants.

> Therefore *God give thee of the dew of heaven*, and the fatness of the earth, and plenty of corn and wine.
>
> —GENESIS 27:28, KJV,
> EMPHASIS ADDED

> And Isaac his father answered and said unto him, Behold, thy dwelling shall be the fatness of the earth, and of *the dew of heaven from above.*
>
> —GENESIS 27:39, KJV,
> EMPHASIS ADDED

> And it came to pass, that at even the quails came up, and covered the camp: and *in the morning the dew* lay round about the host. And when *the dew that lay was gone up, behold, upon the face of the wilderness there lay a small round thing*, as small as the hoar frost on the ground. And when the children of Israel saw it, they said one to another, It is manna: for they wist not what it was. And Moses said unto them, *This is the bread which the Lord hath given you to eat.*
>
> —EXODUS 16:13–15, KJV,
> EMPHASIS ADDED

> And when *the dew fell upon the camp* in the night, the manna fell upon it.
>
> —NUMBERS 11:9, KJV,
> EMPHASIS ADDED,

> And of Joseph he said, *Blessed of the* LORD *be his land*, for the precious things of heaven, *for the dew,* and for the deep that coucheth beneath.
>
> —DEUTERONOMY 33:13, KJV,
> EMPHASIS ADDED

## Showers

Showers mean blessings, new beginnings, and opening of the windows of heaven. They symbolize answered prayer after a long silence or a famine or a drought. It also represents the mercy and kindness of God. It is a time or season of refreshment, transformation, and new dispensation.

> Give ear, O ye heavens, and I will speak; and hear, O earth, the words of my mouth. *My doctrine shall drop as the rain, my speech shall distil as the dew, as the small rain upon the tender herb, and as the showers upon the grass*: Because I will publish the name of the LORD: ascribe ye greatness unto our God.
>
> —DEUTERONOMY 32:1–3, KJV,
> EMPHASIS ADDED

> *Thou visitest the earth, and waterest it*: thou greatly enrichest it with the river of God, which is full of water: thou preparest them corn, when thou hast so provided for it. *Thou waterest the ridges thereof abundantly: thou settlest the furrows thereof: thou makest it soft with showers*: thou blessest the springing thereof.
>
> —PSALMS 65:9–10, KJV,
> EMPHASIS ADDED

Showers of rain also represent restoration and revival.

> And I will make with them a covenant of peace, and will cause the evil beasts to cease out of the land: and they shall dwell safely in the wilderness, and sleep in the woods. And I will make them and the places round about my hill a blessing; *and I will cause the shower to come down in his season; there shall be showers of blessing.* And the tree of the field shall yield her fruit, and the earth shall yield her increase, and they shall be safe in their land, and shall know that I am the LORD, when I have broken the bands of their yoke, and delivered them out of the hand of those that served themselves of them.
>
> —EZEKIEL 34:25–27, KJV,
> EMPHASIS ADDED

## The sea

The sea carries a multiplicity of meanings and interpretations in the realms of the spirit, just as it contains an assortment of materials. It has a broad connotation in the prophetic language and other forms of revelation.

In the natural, the sea is a bundle of abundance in mineral resources and living things. The sea covers the earth. All major rivers travel from the mountains, plains, and valleys to find their ways to flow into the sea. In the process, the sea also has a collection of contents from many waters.

Based on its natural resources and prowess, the sea carries a mixture of symbols, and its nuances also vary according to the circumstances that surround a particular revelation.

The following are some unique gradations that constitute the interpretation of revelation and prophecies that involve the sea:

*The sea as power and authority*

The sea is a symbol of power and authority.

> But lift thou up thy rod, and stretch out thine hand over the sea, and divide it: and the children of Israel shall go on dry ground through the midst of the sea....And Moses stretched out his hand over the sea; and the LORD caused the sea to go back by a strong east wind all that night, and made the sea dry land, and the waters were divided....And Moses stretched forth his hand over the sea, and the sea returned to his strength when the morning appeared; and the Egyptians fled against it; and the LORD overthrew the Egyptians in the midst of the sea.
>
> —EXODUS 14:16, 21, 27, KJV

*The sea as voyaging and merchandising*

The sea represents voyage, business, and variety of blessings.

> Zebulun shall dwell at the haven of the sea; and he shall be for an haven of ships; and his border shall be unto Zidon.
>
> —GENESIS 49:13, KJV

### The seas as wealth and mineral resources

The sea is symbol of wealth and mineral resources. It contains petroleum oil, gas, salt, gold, silver, diamonds, and varieties of precious stones.

> Then thou shalt see, and flow together, and thine heart shall fear, and be enlarged; because the abundance of the sea shall be converted unto thee, the forces of the Gentiles shall come unto thee.
>
> —ISAIAH 60:5, KJV

### The sea as increase and abundance

The sea represents increase and abundance. It harbors living things that provide food for humans and animals; a variety of fishes, crabs, lobster and shrimps abound in the sea.

> And Joseph gathered corn as the sand of the sea, very much, until he left numbering; for it was without number.
>
> —GENESIS 41:49, KJV

> Judah and Israel were many, as the sand which is by the sea in multitude, eating and drinking, and making merry.
>
> —1 KINGS 4:20, KJV

### The sea as evangelism and salvation of souls

The sea represents evangelism and salvation of souls. It also represents increase and multitudes of people.

And thou saidst, I will surely do thee good, and make thy seed as the sand of the sea, which cannot be numbered for multitude.

—GENESIS 32:12, KJV

And they went out, they and all their hosts with them, much people, even as the sand that is upon the sea shore in multitude, with horses and chariots very many.

—JOSHUA 11:4, KJV

*The sea as wisdom and knowledge*

The sea represents a wealth of wisdom and knowledge.

And God gave Solomon wisdom and understanding exceeding much, and largeness of heart, even as the sand that is on the sea shore. And Solomon's wisdom excelled the wisdom of all the children of the east country, and all the wisdom of Egypt.

—1 KINGS 4:29–30, KJV

*The sea as divine protection*

The sea also means divine protection from an enemy.

But God led the people about, through the way of the wilderness of the Red sea: and the children of Israel went up harnessed out of the land of Egypt...Speak unto the children of Israel, that they turn and encamp before Pihahiroth, between Migdol and the sea, over against Baalzephon: before it shall ye encamp by the sea....But the Egyptians pursued after them, all the horses and chariots of

> Pharaoh, and his horsemen, and his army, and over-
> took them encamping by the sea, beside Pihahiroth,
> before Baalzephon.
>
> —EXODUS 13:18; 14:2, 9, KJV

## *The sea as a wall of protection*

The Lord uses the sea to build a wall of protection around his children.

> And the children of Israel went into the midst of the
> sea upon the dry ground: and the waters were a wall
> unto them on their right hand, and on their left...But
> the children of Israel walked upon dry land in the
> midst of the sea; and the waters were a wall unto
> them on their right hand, and on their left.
>
> —EXODUS 14:22, 29, KJV

## *The sea as a border of protection and possession*

The Lord also uses the sea to build a border of protection around the possession He gives to his children.

> And as for the western border, ye shall even have
> the great sea for a border: this shall be your west
> border.
>
> —NUMBERS 34:6, KJV

> And I will set thy bounds from the Red sea even
> unto the sea of the Philistines, and from the desert
> unto the river: for I will deliver the inhabitants of
> the land into your hand; and thou shalt drive them
> out before thee.
>
> —EXODUS 23:31, KJV

> Every place whereon the soles of your feet shall tread
> shall be yours: from the wilderness and Lebanon,
> from the river, the river Euphrates, even unto the
> uttermost sea shall your coast be.
>
> —DEUTERONOMY 11:24, KJV

*The sea as the hand of God*

The sea represents the divine presence of God in a matter. It reveals the powerful hand of God as a sign of miracle. The hand of God means God is about to do something that is beyond human comprehension.

> And it came to pass, when all the kings of the Amor-
> ites, which were on the side of Jordan westward, and
> all the kings of the Canaanites, which were by the
> sea, heard that the LORD had dried up the waters
> of Jordan from before the children of Israel, until
> we were passed over, that their heart melted, neither
> was there spirit in them any more, because of the
> children of Israel.
>
> —JOSHUA 5:1, KJV

*The sea and negative revelations*

Although some revelations connected to the sea may also carry some negative connation, the goodness of it surpasses the evil therein. During the flood that swept the whole world during the era of Noah, all creatures that did not go into the ark with Noah were either destroyed or swept into the sea. It is assumed that some of the evil spirits that copulated with humans during the age of Noah were also swept into the sea. Some powers and principalities of darkness like the mermaid, queen of the coast, leviathan spirit, and the serpentine spirit dwell in water and especially in lakes, rivers, and the sea. Each of these spirits is lust and sex oriented.

> That the sons of God saw the daughters of men that they were fair; and they took them wives of all which they chose.
> —Genesis 6:2, kjv

One of the principalities of darkness that still interferes with humans is the leviathan spirit. The leviathan is one of the spirits that marries men and women in the spirit. Wherever there is a spiritual marriage with the leviathan spirit or the mermaid spirit, the victim will suffer constant sexual interference in dreams. Sometimes ladies who are victims suffer sexual violation and molestation in the natural realm. The men who are victims can sleep with anybody, irrespective of age, sex, or status. No matter the position a man occupies, the leviathan and the mermaid (mermen spirit) possess them so strongly they do not know when they sexually violate family members and babies.

The leviathan spirit is the cause of divorce. Once a leviathan spirit attacks a spouse, there is likely to be a divorce unless the leviathan is driven out through deliverance ministration. The leviathan visits his victims at certain seasons until a marriage is destroyed. The book of Job discusses the tricks of the leviathan and his seductive relationship with humans.

Canst thou draw out leviathan with an hook? or his tongue with a cord which thou lettest down? Canst thou put an hook into his nose? or bore his jaw through with a thorn? Will he make many supplications unto thee? will he speak soft words unto thee? Will he make a covenant with thee? wilt thou take him for a servant for ever? Wilt thou play with him as with a bird? or wilt thou bind him for thy maidens? Shall the companions make a banquet of him? shall they part him among the merchants? Canst thou fill his skin with barbed irons? or his head with fish spears? Lay thine hand upon him, remember the battle, do no more.

—JOB 41:1–8, KJV

In that day the LORD with his sore and great and strong sword shall punish leviathan the piercing serpent, even leviathan that crooked serpent; and he shall slay the dragon that is in the sea.

—ISAIAH 27:1, KJV

## Human Nature and Characteristics

Human nature and characteristics also constitute the prophetic language and interpretation. Human characteristics such as countenance, expression, composure, and emotion are prophetic connotations. Each of these human characteristics has impact and meaning in prophetic undertones.

## Laughter

Laughter is a strong prophetic gradation. There are different types of laughter. Laughter is naturally an expression of excitement. However, it may be given as a sign of joy or a sign of mockery.

### Excitement and celebration

Laughter is usually a sign of joy, excitement, celebration, and good news that attracts a mood for singing, dancing, and jubilation. Laughter is a good omen.

> When the LORD turned again the captivity of Zion, we were like them that dream. Then was our mouth filled with laughter, and our tongue with singing: then said they among the heathen, The LORD hath done great things for them. The LORD hath done great things for us; whereof we are glad.
> —PSALM 126:1–3, KJV

> A feast is made for laughter, and wine maketh merry: but money answereth all things.
> —ECCLESIASTES 10:19, KJV

> Even in laughter the heart is sorrowful; and the end of that mirth is heaviness.
> —PROVERBS 14:13, KJV

### Laughter as mockery

However, there is a type of laughter that is evil. A sinister type of laughter is evil. Sinister laughter is threatening, scary, or intimidating. It is a sign of mockery and satanic jesting.

For as the crackling of thorns under a pot, so is the laughter of the fool: this also is vanity.

—ECCLESIASTES 7:6, KJV

Be afflicted, and mourn, and weep: let your laughter be turned to mourning, and your joy to heaviness.

—JAMES 4:9, KJV

All they that see me laugh me to scorn: they shoot out the lip, they shake the head.

—PSALM 22:7, KJV

### Laughter as a figure of speech

Thou makest us a strife unto our neighbours: and our enemies laugh among themselves.

—PSALM 80:6, KJV

I also will laugh at your calamity; I will mock when your fear cometh.

—PROVERBS 1:26, KJV

If a wise man contendeth with a foolish man, whether he rage or laugh, there is no rest.

—PROVERBS 29:9, KJV

### Laughter as a surprise

Laughter can also be an expression of shock and surprise at an unexpected matter. When Sarah heard the declaration of promise that was being repeated to her husband Abraham, she was overtaken with shock, because her dream and expectation for childbearing had been forgotten.

Sarah was surprised that the Lord was still holding on to the promise He had made. Her mind could not comprehend the fact that a person of her age could still conceive and bear a child. Sarah's laughter was not a case of mockery, but a case of divine embarrassment. Considering her age, she felt that carrying a pregnancy was awkward.

The spiritual concept of Sarah's laughter is embedded in the name of her son, Isaac. *Isaac* means laughter, which can be identified with the expression of shock that oozed out of Sarah when she heard the reinforcement of God's visitation upon her home.

The interpretation of laughter in a prophecy or revelation depends on the environment or phenomenon that fosters it, as in the case of Sarah.

> Therefore Sarah laughed within herself, saying, After I am waxed old shall I have pleasure, my lord being old also? And the LORD said unto Abraham, Wherefore did Sarah laugh, saying, Shall I of a surety bear a child, which am old? Is any thing too hard for the LORD? At the time appointed I will return unto thee, according to the time of life, and Sarah shall have a son.
>
> —GENESIS 18:12–14, KJV

*Crying and weeping*

Crying and weeping are expressions of pain or sorrow. Jeremiah wept for the impending captivity of Israel, but no one understood him. Crying can mean anything from the issue of pain or sorrow to a call for help, mercy, repentance, forgiveness, or for divine intervention.

# Chapter 9

# PROPHETIC DELIVERANCE

THIS CHAPTER ON prophetic deliverance focuses on the core and purpose of this book. The discussion of this topic is strategically scheduled for this chapter in order to take readers from the periphery into the heart of the matter that causes challenges and difficulties to demand the attention of deliverance ministration at a prophetic level. (The discussion on prophetic deliverance will continued in the next book, *School of Prophet: II*)

## Job Description

As we embark on the discussion on prophetic deliverance, it is important that we define the heart of the subject matter—deliverance. The focus of this book is not a study of the general function of the prophetic office, but rather the specialized area of the prophetic ministry. There is a medical office that performs a basic function, and there is a specialized medical office that focuses on specific area of health care. Similarly, there is a prophetic office that is general and there is a specialized office in the prophetic realm that focuses on providing solutions to specific needs.

This author specializes in her area of divine assignment, which is prophetic deliverance. When God calls you, He also provides you with a job description to enable you perform your duty with some level of expertise and specialization. The previous chapters of this book have discussed topics that pertained to some of the issues we encountered during deliverance ministration. The chapters also provided answers to some of the questions that are posed at the School of Deliverance held in different parts of the world and at home in New York.

In view of these matters, it is necessary that we deal with the definition of terms that relates to a call, an office, and job description. This procedure will enable readers to understand and appreciate the solutions provided by this book in the realms of prophetic deliverance.

## The Deliverance Ministry

### What is deliverance?

Deliverance is the process of getting out of a problem and stepping into a solution. It is a manner of disentangling oneself from an entanglement. It is a procedure of moving out of darkness into light.

The problem that needs deliverance ministration may be spiritual, physical, emotional, material, financial, or secular. Deliverance is also the manner of renouncing any affiliation with the demonic world and forming an alliance with Christ Jesus. It is the process of separating from anything that pollutes or contaminates one's relationship with the Lord Jesus Christ.

There are different types of deliverance ministrations. All deliverances are not the same, and all problems needing deliverance ministration are not related to demon possession. This author has written several books on deliverance ministrations. In order not to repeat what has already been published in other books, be encouraged to request the following titles: *Receive and Maintain Your Deliverance on Legal Grounds, Pulling Down Satanic Strongholds, When Satan Went to Church,* and *Solution: Deliverance Ministration to Self and Others.* See the section on "Books Written by Pauline Walley-Daniels" for details.

### What is deliverance ministration?

Deliverance ministration is the act of assisting others or self to either separate from an affiliation with a demonic spirit or from satanic interferences. Deliverance ministration can be carried out by counseling the victim and also commanding the interfering spirit to exit from an individual.

There are seven levels of deliverance ministrations, out of which the four major levels of ministrations are presented below:

**The first level** is the knowledge and understanding of the importance of confession, repentance, and forgiveness of sin.

**The second level** is applying the procedure of atonement to one's daily life to prevent further invasion by familiar spirits.

**The third level** is separating oneself from demonic entities to which one holds a type of affiliation consciously and unconsciously.

**The fourth level** is casting out demons and uprooting satanic trees from one's life by the help of others.

## The Prophetic Ministry

### What is prophecy?

Prophecy is speaking forth the Word of the Lord that is received through revelation or direct unction. Prophecy is releasing divine utterance by the unction of the Holy Spirit. A prophecy may concern a person, a people, nation, or a place directly or indirectly. It may relate to the past, present, or future.

## What is a word of prophecy?

A word of prophecy is a specific message or Word of God delivered by a person who occupies the office of a prophet. Although a word of prophecy may be general, more often than not, a word of prophecy from an anointed prophet of God is usually very specific and purpose oriented.

## What is a gift of prophecy?

A gift of prophecy is an inspirational unction that makes a person speak out an unknown matter out of unconsciousness, either regularly or occasionally. The matter released from the gift of prophecy is often very general. It is meant to edify or build up, exhort or encourage, and comfort or console and heal. Sometimes individuals that exercise the occasional gift of prophecy want to instruct and direct the church by dramatizing unconsciousness in this realm.

I once attended a fellowship where people used the gift of prophecy to control the activities of the church. I noticed that the gentlemen in that fellowship were not bold enough to propose marriage to the ladies. The adopted system was to share a desire with someone who exercised the gift of prophecy. During a prayer meeting, someone with the gift of prophecy would suddenly slump into a state of unconsciousness and begin to give directions to a sister to marry a particular brother. In many churches the gift of prophecy has been wrongly used to manipulate ministers and leaders to succumb to wishes and desires that would not receive normal attention. Similarly, people have used this gift as a means to express their feelings by pretending to teach or preach in a state of unconsciousness.

The gift of prophecy that is exercised by a person that is not operating in the office of a prophet is not usually meant to instruct, direct, teach, or preach in any form. But a person operating in the office of a prophet can instruct, direct, teach, and preach under an inspirational state of unconsciousness. Everyone exercising the gift of prophecy is not necessarily a prophet. A person fulfilling the office of a prophet can exercise the gift of prophecy as an inspirational enhancement.

### What is prophetic ministration?

Prophetic ministration is the act of delivering a message of the Lord with an additional responsibility to perform some other specific assignments, such as making appointments, praying, or interceding for the person or people concerned as instructed by the Holy Spirit. The prophetic message is delivered either by direct utterance or by performing a specific duty according to the direction of the Holy Spirit and also one's regular job description.

Samuel was a prophet whose duties extended beyond performing basic functions. He was also a priest and a kingmaker. He anointed both Saul and David as kings over Israel.

> Now the Lord had told Samuel in his ear a day before Saul came, saying, To morrow about this time I will send thee a man out of the land of Benjamin, and thou shalt anoint him to be captain over my people Israel, that he may save my people from the hand of the Philistines: for I have looked upon my

people, because their cry has come to me. And when
Samuel saw Saul, the Lord said to him, Behold the
man whom I spoke to thee of! this same shall reign
over my people....Then Samuel took a vial of oil,
and poured it upon his head, and kissed him, and
said, Is it not because the Lord hath anointed thee to
be captain over his inheritance?

—1 SAMUEL 9:15–17; 10:1, KJV,
EMPHASIS ADDED

In the realm of prophetic ministration, the person
who delivers the prophetic message carries a burden of
intercession for the recipient. Thus, besides delivering a
message, the prophet prays with the recipient based on the
Word of the Lord that has come forth.

The prophetic word is also delivered by giving directives and instructions to the recipient. Samuel listened
carefully to divine instructions and followed every detailed
directive that was connected to the prophetic assignments
that the Lord sent him to implement.

And the LORD said to Samuel, *How long wilt thou
mourn for Saul, seeing I have rejected him from
reigning over Israel? Fill thy horn with oil, and go,
I will send thee to Jesse the Bethlehemite: for I have
provided me a king among his sons.* And Samuel
said, How can I go? if Saul shall hear it, he will kill
me. And the LORD said, *Take a heifer with thee, and
say, I have come to sacrifice to the LORD.* And *call
Jesse to the sacrifice, and I will show thee what thou
shalt do: and thou shalt anoint to me him whom I*

*name to thee. And Samuel did that which the* LORD *spoke,* and came to Bethlehem. And the elders of the town trembled at his coming, and said, Comest thou peaceably? And he said, Peaceably: I have come to sacrifice to the LORD: sanctify yourselves, and come with me to the sacrifice. *And he sanctified Jesse and his sons, and called them to the sacrifice.*

And it came to pass when they had come, that he looked on Eliab, and said, Surely the LORD's anointed is before him. But the LORD said to Samuel, Look not on his countenance, or on the height of his stature; because I have refused him: for the LORD seeth not as man seeth; *for man looketh on the outward appearance, but the* LORD *looketh on the heart.* Then Jesse called Abinadab, and made him pass before Samuel. And he said, Neither hath the LORD chosen this. Then Jesse made Shammah to pass by. And he said, Neither hath the LORD chosen this. Again, *Jesse made seven of his sons to pass before Samuel. And Samuel said to Jesse, The* LORD *hath not chosen these.* And *Samuel said to Jesse, Are here all thy children?* And he said, *There remaineth yet the youngest,* and behold, he keepeth the sheep. And Samuel said to Jesse, Send and fetch him: for we will not sit down till he hath come hither. And he sent, and brought him in. *Now he was ruddy, and also of a beautiful countenance, and a goodly to look to. And the* LORD *said, Arise, anoint him: for this is he. Then Samuel took the horn of oil, and anointed him in the midst of his brethren: and the Spirit of the* LORD *came upon David from that day forward.* So Samuel arose, and went to Ramah.

*But the Spirit of the LORD departed from Saul, and an evil spirit from the LORD troubled him.* And Saul's servants said to him, Behold now, an evil spirit from God troubleth thee. Let our lord now command thy servants, which are before thee, to seek a man, who is a cuning player on a harp: and it shall come to pass, when the evil spirit from God is upon thee, that he will play with his hand, and thou wilt be well. And Saul said to his servants, Provide me now a man that can play well, and bring him to me. Then answered one of the servants, and said, *Behold, I have seen a son of Jesse the Bethlehemite, that is cunning in playing, and a mighty valiant man, and a man of war, and prudent in matters, and a comely person, and the LORD is with him.* Wherefore Saul sent messengers to Jesse, and said, *Send me David thy son*, which is with the sheep. And Jesse took an ass laden with bread, and a bottle of wine, and a kid, and sent them by David his son to Saul. And David came to Saul, and stood before him: and he loved him greatly; and he became his armourbearer. *And Saul sent to Jesse, saying, Let David, I pray thee, stand before me; for he hath found favour in my sight. And it came to pass, when the evil spirit from God was upon Saul, that David took a harp, and played with his hand: so Saul was refreshed, and was well, and the evil spirit departed from him.*

—1 SAMUEL 16:1–23, KJV,
EMPHASIS ADDED

Ministration is necessary when a prophetic message carries a burden for repentance, forgiveness, or confession of sin. That means the recipient needs help to change his or her ways or lifestyle of compromise. It means the recipient indulges in some type of sin or unforgiveness and needs to be pulled out from the realms of darkness into the realms of righteousness. When light comes, darkness must go. Therefore, when a prophecy carries a notion of sin or waywardness, there is a need to salvage the situation by bringing the individual concerned to the foot of the cross for repentance. This level of ministration may require counseling with the recipient. It is a type of prophetic ministration with a focus on counseling.

John 1:1–5 (KJV) tells us:

> In the beginning was the Word, and the Word was with God, and the Word was God. The same was in the beginning with God. All things were made by him; and without him was not any thing made that was made. In him was life; and the life was the light of men. And the light shineth in darkness; and the darkness comprehended it not.

Also, prophetic ministration is important when the recipient is heartbroken from disappointment, failure, oppression, frustration, depression, or suppression. It is not enough for a prophet to give a word that identifies the state of the recipient as having suffered brokenheartedness. In prophetic ministration, the prophet goes on to deal with the situation as led by the Lord to bring total restoration into the life of the victim.

It is important to note that all persons who function

in the prophetic do not perform the same type of duties. Some are called to execute basic duties of delivering a message, while others are assigned to operate other ministerial functions according to their job descriptions and specialties. For instance, one of the reasons the Lord rejected Saul from being the king of Israel was because he executed a duty that was not assigned to him.

Saul executed the role of the priest when he performed an unlawful sacrifice. "And Saul said, Bring hither a burnt offering to me, and peace offerings. And he offered the burnt offering" (1 Sam. 13:9, KJV).

Following the act of interfering with a priestly duty that was not divinely assigned to him, Saul suffered the repercussion of transgressing the law of the Most High God. The Lord sent Samuel to reprimand Saul with a message that carried a weight of judgment.

> And Samuel said to Saul, *Thou hast done foolishly: thou hast not kept the commandment of the LORD thy God, which he commanded thee*: for now would the LORD have established thy kingdom upon Israel for ever. But now *thy kingdom shall not continue*: the LORD hath sought him a man after his own heart, and the LORD hath commanded him to be captain over his people, because thou hast not kept that which the LORD commanded thee.
> —1 SAMUEL 13:13-14, KJV,
> EMPHASIS ADDED

Hence, David was anointed king while Saul was still on the throne.

Then came the word of the LORD to Samuel, saying, *It repenteth me that I have set up Saul to be king: for he is turned back from following me, and hath not performed my commandments.* And *it grieved Samuel; and he cried to the LORD all night.* And when Samuel rose early to meet Saul in the morning, it was told Samuel, saying, Saul came to Carmel, and behold, he set him up a place, and has gone about, and passed on, and gone down to Gilgal. And Samuel came to Saul: and Saul said to him, Blessed be thou of the LORD: I have performed the commandment of the LORD. And Samuel said, What meaneth then this bleating of the sheep in my ears, and the lowing of the oxen which I hear? And Saul said, They have brought them from the Amalekites: for the people spared the best of the sheep and of the oxen, to sacrifice to the LORD thy God; and the rest we have utterly destroyed. Then Samuel said to Saul, Stay, and I will tell thee what the LORD hath said to me this night. And he said to him, Say on. And Samuel said, *When thou wast little in thy own sight, wast thou not made the head of the tribes of Israel, and the LORD anointed thee king over Israel? And the LORD sent thee on a journey, and said, Go, and utterly destroy the sinners the Amalekites, and fight against them until they are consumed. Wherefore then didst thou not obey the voice of the LORD, but didst fly upon the spoil, and didst evil in the sight of the LORD?*

—1 SAMUEL 15:10–19, KJV,

EMPHASIS ADDED

In recent times there have been infiltration and interferences with ministries and ministers everywhere. Many have not been able to stay within their calling because they do not understand the importance of their calling and job description. Ministries are splitting up and many who have no vision of their own are copying what they see others do. Almost every minister wants to have an itinerant ministry. Many are bearing titles they do not understand and performing duties they watched and copied from television programs.

If you are sent with a message that requires an implementation of a responsibility that is not within your jurisdiction of duty, it is wise to refer the recipient to seek ministration at an appropriate quarter. Do not try to execute a responsibility that God has not assigned to you.

> Now there are *diversities of gifts*, but the *same Spirit*. And there are *differences of administrations*, but the *same Lord*. And there are *diversities of operations*, but it is the *same God who worketh all in all*. But the manifestation of the Spirit is given to every man for profit.
> —1 CORINTHIANS 12:4–7, KJV,
> EMPHASIS ADDED

### What is prophetic deliverance ministration?

Prophetic deliverance is the manner of receiving and releasing a word from the Lord that is healing or deliverance oriented. It is an instant manifestation of a prophetic word that exposes the work of the enemy in order to set the captive free, release those in bondage, and pull down satanic strongholds.

The healing or deliverance involved in prophetic deliverance ministration may be spiritual, physical, emotional, material, financial, or secular. Prophetic deliverance is signs and wonders or miracle oriented. It is an instant performance of the Word of the Lord as it is being spoken.

Joseph was a prophetic deliverer for the nation of Egypt and the children of Israel. He brought forth prophetic deliverance by the word of wisdom to his fellow prisoners through interpretation of revelations and they were released. Subsequently, his ministry spread beyond the walls of the prison to the palace of Pharaoh. (See Genesis 40:6–13.)

*Prophetic deliverance from poverty*

Poverty is a state of lack, insufficiency, penury, deficiency, paucity, scarcity, and economic failure. There are different types of poverty related to the realms of human existence and the territory where humans dwell. Both individuals and organizations may suffer any form of poverty in the spiritual, physical, natural, emotional, material, secular, or financial realm. Poverty is a spirit that attacks anything that has substance in it, including human beings, lands, trees, institutions, and a region or a country.

Prophetic deliverance from poverty means God has shown a prophet how the spirit of poverty is interfering with a victim. The revelation goes further to expose the type of poverty and how it attacks a victim. The Lord will also show the prophet how to take some specific steps to follow in order to cast out that particular spirit so that the victim would be freed.

*Prophetic deliverance over the nation of Egypt*

Pharaoh, the king of Egypt, received a revelation through a dream concerning what would happen in his territory. Although the dream he had troubled him, he did not know the interpretation of it. So he sought for an interpreter of dream to help him solve the riddles of his revelation.

When Pharaoh narrated his dream, Joseph did not only interpret the dream that meant economic failure, but also gave specific instructions as to how the puzzle of Pharaoh's dream could be solved. The manner of Joseph's interpretation and presentation is an act of prophetic deliverance. Thus Joseph did not only revealed that there was going to be an economic failure and insolvency in the nation, but also gave solutions to how to arrest the impending hardships that would follow an era of abundance.

Joseph performed prophetic deliverance ministration on Pharaoh by giving him specific instructions: how to appoint officers and the job descriptions that would enable the officers to perform their duties efficiently so that the famine which represented a type of poverty would not destroy the land Egypt.

> And for that the dream was doubled to Pharaoh twice; it is because the thing is established by God, and God will shortly bring it to pass. Now therefore

let Pharaoh look out a man discreet and wise, and set him over the land of Egypt. Let Pharaoh do this, and let him appoint officers over the land, and take up the fifth part of the land of Egypt in the seven plenteous years. And let them gather all the food of those good years that come, and lay up corn under the hand of Pharaoh; and let them keep food in the cities. And that food shall be for store to the land against the seven years of famine, which shall be in the land of Egypt; that the land may not perish through the famine. And the thing was good in the eyes of Pharaoh, and in the eyes of all his servants.

—GENESIS 41:32–37, KJV,
EMPHASIS ADDED

While Joseph was still speaking, Pharaoh began to receive his deliverance from the fears and depression that his dreams had brought to him. The prophetic interpretation that Joseph gave released him, and he was instantly delivered. Following his deliverance, Pharaoh honored Joseph by placing him in a high-ranking position that was next to his kingship authority.

And Pharaoh said to his servants, *Can we find such a man as this is, a man in whom the spirit of God is?* And Pharaoh said to Joseph, Forasmuch as God hath shown thee all this, *there is none so discreet and wise as thou art: Thou shalt be over my house, and according to thy word shall all my people be ruled: only in the throne will I be greater than thou.* And Pharaoh said to Joseph, *See, I have set thee over all the land of Egypt. And Pharaoh took off his ring from his hand, and put it upon Joseph's hand, and arrayed him in vestures of fine linen, and put a gold chain about his neck;* And he made him to ride in the second chariot which he had: and they cried before him, Bow the knee: *and he made him ruler over all the land of Egypt.* And Pharaoh said to Joseph, I am Pharaoh, and without thee shall no man lift up his hand or foot in all the land of Egypt.

—GENESIS 41:38–44, KJV,
EMPHASIS ADDED

Joseph was promoted by an earthly king because he demonstrated the fear of God in all his endeavors even when all odds were against him. He did not allow distractions and other people's behavior to interfere with his relationship with the Most High God. He did just what the Holy Spirit led him to do. Hence, he was successful and blessed.

Other prophets that performed prophetic deliverance ministration in the Bible include Elisha and Daniel.

*Prophetic deliverance from financial debt*

A person or an organization or nation may be wealthy in resources but can still go into debt or enter a state of bankruptcy because of financial mismanagement or demonic attack.

Elisha operated in the realms of prophetic deliverance in the case of a widow. Elisha ministered prophetic deliverance that brought a financial solution to the widow and her family who were in a state of bankruptcy due to the death of the head of the home—probably the breadwinner for the family. Although the woman was suffering penury because of the death of her husband, she had a treasure that could provide her some money. But for the divine intervention of the Elisha, the widow did not know the worth of her treasure. Besides the material wealth of oil in her home, the widow was also rich in spirit. She was wealthy in character and rich in the spirit of obedience. She understood the voice of authority and respected the utterance of the prophet.

Elisha gave the widow a specific instruction, which was a word of deliverance. The deliverance was manifested because the widow obeyed the prophetic instructions given to her.

When the widow cried out to him for help in connection to her sons, Elisha did not just prophesy blessings of abundance, but gave the woman an instruction. The woman's positive response to the prophet's instruction led to her complete deliverance of her children from slavery.

> Now there cried a certain woman of the wives of the sons of the prophets unto Elisha, saying, Thy servant my husband is dead; and thou knowest that thy servant did fear the LORD: and *the creditor is come to take unto him my two sons to be bondmen.* And Elisha said unto her, *What shall I do for thee?* tell me, *what hast thou in the house?* And she said, Thine handmaid hath not any thing in the house, save a pot of oil. Then he said, *Go, borrow thee vessels abroad of all thy neighbours, even empty vessels; borrow not a few. And when thou art come in, thou shalt shut*

*the door upon thee and upon thy sons, and shalt pour out into all those vessels, and thou shalt set aside that which is full.* So she went from him, and shut the door upon her and upon her sons, who brought the vessels to her; and she poured out. And it came to pass, when the vessels were full, that she said unto her son, Bring me yet a vessel. And he said unto her, There is not a vessel more. And the oil stayed. *Then she came and told the man of God. And he said, Go, sell the oil, and pay thy debt, and live thou and thy children of the rest.*

—2 Kings 4:1–7, kjv,
EMPHASIS ADDED

### Prophetic deliverance from leprosy

Leprosy brings a state of shame, disgrace, embarrassment, and rejection. Leprosy is a disease that eats up the fingers and toes of its victim. Victims of leprosy are usually isolated or cast out of their family or society. Lepers are not allowed to socialize with the public. Sometimes people suffer from moral situations that put them in the state of a leper.

It is amazing that Naaman was permitted to carry on his job as the commander of the Syrian army. This probably happened because there was nobody else to fill his position. Sometimes people come into situations that should require ostracizing from their duty or position, but they are still being kept because there are not too many choices for filling their position or duty. In certain quarters, the people that need some sort of discipline are too high or proud to submit to authority or discipline, so they continue their duties despite their state of "leprosy."

Probably Naaman was allowed to continue in his position because he was humble and ready for healing, although he initially refused to obey the prophet's instruction when he was told to go and wash in the river Jordan. He, however, submitted when he understood the explanation given to him.

Elisha performed prophetic deliverance on Naaman, the commander of the Syrian Army, by instructing him to go wash in the Jordan seven times. Although Naaman was a mighty man of valor, he suffered from leprosy. Elisha gave Naaman an instruction that was to release him from the spirit of leprosy. The instruction given to Naaman was a prophetic word for healing and deliverance.

> And Elisha sent a messenger to him, saying, *Go and wash in Jordan seven times, and thy flesh shall come again to thee, and thou shalt be clean.* But *Naaman was wroth, and went away, and said, Behold, I thought, He will surely come out to me, and stand, and call on the name of the* LORD *his God, and strike his hand over the place, and recover the leper.* Are not Abana and Pharpar, rivers of Damascus, better than all the waters of Israel? may I not wash in them, and be clean? So he turned and went away in a rage. And *his servants came near, and spoke to him, and said, My father, if the prophet had bid thee do some great thing, wouldst thou not have done it? how much rather then, when he saith to thee, Wash, and be clean? Then he went down, and dipped himself seven*

*times in Jordan, according to the saying of the man of God: and his flesh came again like the flesh of a little child, and he was clean.* And he returned to the man of God, he and all his company, and came and stood before him: and he said, *Behold, now I know that there is no God in all the earth, but in Israel:* now therefore, I pray thee, take a blessing from thy servant.

—2 KINGS 5:10–15, KJV,
EMPHASIS ADDED

*Prophetic deliverance from the spirit of death*

During one of his teaching sessions at the School of Prophets, there was a need for Elisha to demonstrate prophetic deliverance to the prophets in training. The sons of the prophets cooked a stew with some herbs that turned out to be poisonous. The students then cried out to Elisha for deliverance and the power of death was nullified and the food was purified for consumption.

And Elisha came again to Gilgal. And *there was a dearth in the land*; and the sons of the prophets were sitting before him: and he said to his servant, *Set on the great pot, and seethe pottage for the sons of the prophets. And one went out into the field to gather herbs, and found a wild vine, and gathered from it wild gourds his lap full, and came and shred them into the pot of pottage: for they knew them not.* So they poured out for the men to eat. *And it came to pass, as they were eating of the pottage, that they cried out, and said, O thou man of God, there is death in the pot.* And they could not eat of it. But he said,

*Then bring meal. And he cast it into the pot; and he said, Pour out for the people, that they may eat. And there was no harm in the pot.*

—2 KINGS 4:38–41, KJV,
EMPHASIS ADDED

In another development, a Shunammite woman's son died. When the woman approached Elisha for help, he sent his armor bearer Gehazi with his scepter of authority to minister to the child. But Gehazi could not cast out the spirit of death, so Elisha went and performed the deliverance ministration.

And when she came to the man of God to the hill, she caught him by the feet: but Gehazi came near to thrust her away. And the man of God said, *Let her alone; for her soul is sorrowful within her: and the LORD hath hid it from me, and hath not told me. Then she said, Did I ask a son from my lord? did I not say, Do not deceive me. Then he said to Gehazi, Gird up thy loins and take my staff in thy hand,* and go thy way: and if thou shalt meet any man, salute him not; and if any shall salute thee, answer him not again: *and lay my staff upon the face of the child.* And the mother of the child said, As the LORD liveth, and as thy soul liveth, I will not leave thee. And he arose, and followed her. *And Gehazi passed on before them, and laid the staff upon the face of the child; but there was neither voice, nor hearing.* Wherefore he went again to meet him, and told him, saying, The child is not awaked. *And when Elisha had come into the house, behold, the child was dead, and laid upon his bed. He went in therefore, and shut the door upon them both, and prayed to the Lord. And he went up, and lay upon the child, and put his mouth upon his mouth, and his eyes upon his eyes, and his hands upon his hands: and he stretched himself upon the child; and the flesh of the child waxed warm.* Then he returned, and walked in the house to and fro; and went up, and stretched himself upon him: *and the child sneezed seven times, and the child opened his eyes.* And he called Gehazi, and said, *Call this Shunamite.* So he called her. *And when she had come in to him, he said, Take up thy son.*

—2 Kings 4:27–36, kjv,
EMPHASIS ADDED

*Prophetic deliverance—instruction oriented*

Prophetic deliverance operates strongly on the grounds of instruction. A person who is not submissive to authority cannot carry out prophetic deliverance successfully. A person who is not inclined to following simple instructions from parents, siblings, friends, colleagues, or spouse would find it difficult to listen carefully to divine directions. People who prefer to talk rather listen are not inclined to follow instructions, because they lack the ability to hear what is said at a particular time.

For instance, how can you hear from God who is Spirit and divine when you are not able to listen and hear what a fellow human being is saying to you? It is important that anyone who wants to truly fulfill a prophet ministry learn to pay attention to simple instructions. Once you miss the details of instructions given to you at a particular time, the mission involved will likely fail.

The Biblical prophets like Moses, Elijah, and Elisha were successful in their ministry because they paid attention to the details of instructions given to them. Moses was able to take the children of Israel out of the land of Egypt because he understood the voice of authority and paid attention to instruction details. Based on his submission to authority, he was able to follow every direction that he received to deliver the children of Israel from bondage.

Consequently, Moses was also able to elaborate on the Ten Commandments because he paid attention to the voice of God. Many people do not take time to listen to the whole message. They rush ahead with only a half message, and end up misleading people because they did not hear the whole message and the instruction on how to do it.

When the people disobeyed the authority of God and Moses the leader, their days in the wilderness were prolonged and their promises were delayed. Forty days was multiplied to forty years.

At another level of disobedience, the life of Aaron and his ministry was cut short. Aaron's anointing was transferred to Eleazar his son. Moses also could not step onto the Promised Land because he was angry and struck the rock instead of speaking to it according to divine instruction. Moses's anointing was transferred to Joshua.

Noah heard both the message and the instructions on how to build the ark. He also heard the directives on how to bring his family and the animals and birds into the ark at a particular date and time. Because Noah listened attentively, he was able to accomplish the divine assignments that preserved his life and the others in the ark.

Beloved, do not try to be a prophet because you want to feel good. Listen carefully and follow simple instructions. Be submissive to authority and obedient to rules and regulations. Respect and honor people in authority and you will be blessed.

This discussion will continue in the next book, *School of Prophetic Deliverance II.*

# Decision

If you have never surrendered your life to Jesus Christ as your Lord and Savior, then it would be good for you to do so right away. Otherwise it will be difficult for you to rule over anger and the negatives ruling your life. If you are willing to accept Jesus Christ as your Lord and Savior, then pray like this:

> *Lord Jesus, I come to You just as I am. Forgive me for my sins and deliver me from all works of iniquity. Deliver me from all the evil characteristics and behaviors that have kept me in bondage. Set my soul and spirit free to worship You in spirit and in truth. Come into my life and make me whole. I need You, Lord. I need You every hour into eternity. Amen.*

# Rededication

If you have ever made a decision to surrender your life to Jesus Christ, yet you have been struggling with the Christian life or are somehow an active Christian still struggling with some ungodly characteristics and behaviors, then you need to rededicate yourself to the lordship of your Jesus. Make a total surrender so that the enemy will not have any form of control at all in your life. You may pray like this:

> Lord Jesus, teach me to surrender my total being to Your lordship and control, so that the enemy will no longer have a part in me. Teach me to abide in You so that You will also abide in me and dwell in my life. Teach me to study Your Word and make a conscious effort to apply it to my daily living. Wash me, cleanse me, and purify my spirit, soul, and body that I may be acceptable in Your sight. Thank You, Lord, for delivering me from the works of iniquity. Amen.

Thank you for reading this book.

God bless you.

# BIBLIOGRAPHY

Bickle, Mike. *Growing in the Prophetic.* Lake Mary, FL: Creation House, 1996.

Hamon, Bill. *Apostles Prophets and the Coming Moves of God.* Shippensburg, PA: Destiny Image, 1997.

Sumrall, Lester. *The Gifts & Ministries of the Holy Spirit.* Springdale, PA: Whitaker House, 1993.

VanGemeren, Willem A. *Interpreting the Prophetic Word.* Grand Rapids, MI: Zondervan Publishing House, 1990.

# BOOKS BY DR. PAULINE WALLEY-DANIELS

**About** *School of Prophetic Deliverance*

Everyone believes that he or she is a child of God. Unfortunately, everyone does not hear the voice of the Father and not all are close to Him. Yet all are seeking His divine attention. This book teaches on the basic principles of the prophetic ministry and also gives the basic understanding of the prophetic word and its operations. The understanding of the prophetic word will draw you closer to Him as never before. Stay blessed and enjoy the prophetic realm.

## *The Authority of an Overcomer: You Can Have It, I Have It*

*The Authority of an Overcomer* shares the real-life testimony of a day-to-day experience with the Lord Jesus Christ. It encourages you to apply the Word of God to every facet of your life, such as sleeping and waking with Jesus, walking and talking with Jesus, and dining with Him as you would with your spouse or a friend.

### Somebody Cares, Cares for You, Cares for Me

*Somebody Cares, Cares for You, Cares for Me* talks about the care that the Lord Almighty has for every one of us. It teaches you to care for other people and exercise tolerance towards their shortcomings. You will learn the importance and the true meaning of love as you read this book.

### Receive and Maintain Your Deliverance on Legal Grounds

Many people go from one prayer house to another, from the general practitioner to the specialist, from one minister to the pope, and from one chapel to another church with the same mission—aiming for the same expectation, yet never hitting the target. Why? Many people lack the knowledge of maintaining their healing and deliverance. This book, *Receive and Maintain Your Deliverance on Legal Grounds*, will teach you to understand how to maintain what you receive from God.

### Anger: Get Rid of It, You Can Overcome It

Anger is one of the problems that many seek to resolve but lack the solution. Many have resigned their fate to it, thinking that it is a natural phenomenon. This book teaches about the causes of anger and how to uproot them to receive your healing.

### The Power of the Spoken Word

There is a purpose for which we speak, and when we speak, we expect something to happen in order for the purpose of the utterance to be fulfilled. This book teaches you to exercise your authority so that the word you speak will be manifested effectively.

### The Holy Spirit: The Uniqueness of His Presence

The presence of the Holy Spirit highlights the difference between the gifts of the Spirit, the presence of God, and the visitation of the Holy Spirit. In this book you will learn to enjoy the delightful presence of the Holy Spirit in your spiritual walk.

### The Holy Spirit: Maintain His Presence in Trials and Temptations

This book teaches you how to maintain the presence of God, especially in trials and temptations. Oftentimes when Christians go through difficult situations, they think they are alone. But that need not be. You can enter the presence of the Holy Spirit in difficult times and witness His power to strengthen you and turn your situations around.

### The Holy Spirit: Power of the Tongue

In recent times, many people have been seeking instant power and prophetic manifestations. Christians and ministers are indulging in all sorts of practices to demonstrate some special abilities to attract public attention. This book, *The Holy Spirit: Power of the Tongue*, discusses the various powers and anointings at work. It will help you to decipher between the Holy Spirit power and satanic powers. It will also teach you about the various anointings that exist and how you can reach out for the genuine one.

## *Pulling Down Satanic Strongholds: War Against Evil Spirits*

Many Christians are under satanic attacks and influences, but very few people understand what the actual problems are. Some believe in God, but have no idea that there is anything like the satanic realm, yet they are under satanic torment. This book, *Pulling Down Satanic Strongholds*, enlightens you on some of the operations of the devil. It will help you know when an activity being performed around you is of the devil. This knowledge will strengthen you in prayer and equip you against the wiles of the enemy.

## *When Satan Went to Church*

Many people fear the devil more than they fear God. At the mention of Satan or demons, they are threatened. Yet they are complacent in their own ways and yield to sin easily. Let the fear of God grip you and not the fear of Satan. This book enlightens you on the activities of the enemy within and around the church, the home, and the Christian community. It helps you to identify battles and to put on your armor of warfare against the enemy. It also encourages you to hold firm the shield of faith. May the Lord enlighten your eyes of understanding as you read this book.

## *Solution: Deliverance Ministration to Self and Others*

Since the death of Jesus Christ on the cross, humans have been given the opportunity to experience and encounter the joy of salvation. However, lack of knowledge has kept the world in the dark and deprived them of the importance of Christianity. This book, *Solution: Deliverance Ministration to Self and Others* portrays just what the title says. It teaches you to understand the intricacies of deliverance ministration and to avoid the dangerous practices that have discouraged others. Read it and you will be blessed and informed.

### Strategic Prayer Tactics I: Effective Communications With Aromatic Expressions

This book, *Strategic Prayer Tactics I*, with focus on types and approaches to prayer, teaches you how to approach the throne of God with specific needs and the strategies to adopt for presentation. It also teaches you to pray with Scripture as your legal authority.

### Strategic Prayer Tactics II: Types of Prayer and Tactical Approach

This book teaches you how to approach the throne of God. Prayer is communication between God and man. You will learn the different types of prayer that are mentioned in the Bible. Therefore, your daily endeavors will no longer be a struggle because you will know and understand the meaning of prayer and how to pray with Scriptures as a legal authority. After reading this book your prayer life will change and you will begin to pray more effectively.

### Strategic Prayer Tactics III: Types of Prayer With Aromatic Expressions

This book, *Strategic Prayer Tactics III*, with focus on types of prayer with aromatic expressions, teaches you how to approach the throne of God with a unique offering that attracts divine attention. It also teaches you to be sensitive in the presence of God.

### School of Mentoring and Leadership I: The Act of Mentoring

*The Act of Mentoring* is for stirring up, activating, and imparting talents and abilities for effectiveness. Everyone has talents and abilities that need to be developed in order for a person to achieve an ambition. Many people are bedeviled by unfulfilled dreams and are wallowing in familiar oppression and depression. This book will help you to locate and choose a mentor who will help you to discover and develop your abilities that will lead you into fulfilling your ambition. This course will teach and draw you closer to your destiny. Stay blessed and enjoy the act of mentoring.

### School of Mentoring and Leadership II: Progressive Achievement—Receive It; Maintain It

This book teaches you how to mentor yourself while you move in progression to overcome obstacles that would usually frustrate prosperity. It enlightens you about the various types of progress that may come your way and how to manage them. It also encourages you to overcome failure and disappointment. The book helps you to understand the concept of self-mentoring in the course of progressiveness as part of the characteristics of the Holy Spirit.

All books listed are available in bookstores, by order, and on-line at: www.paulinewalley.org.

# PAULINE WALLEY SCHOOL OF INTENSIVE TRAINING

## for Ministry and Leadership Equipment

## (PW-SITME)

The Pauline Walley School of Intensive Training for Ministry and Leadership Equipment is an institution for training leaders, individuals, and church groups. It is an intensive practical training center where people are taught to build their image and personality, improve their ministry skills and abilities, develop their talents and gifts, and minister to self, family members, friends, and church or fellowship members. In the process of training, people are also taught to be equipped for ministration and to face the battle of life as it is in the ministry.

The areas of study are:

- School of Deliverance (SOD)

- School of Prophetic Deliverance (SPD)

- School of Prophetic Intercession (SPI)

- School of Strategic Prayer (SSP)

- School of Tactical Evangelism (STE)

- School of Mentoring and Leadership (SML)

- School of the Gifts of the Holy Spirit (SGHS)

- School of the Prophets (SOP)

The Pauline Walley School of Intensive Training programs are organized and held in different parts of the world at various times. At seminar levels, one week or two weeks of intensive training are organized to help leaders and ministers or church or fellowship groups to establish various arms of church ministry and also equip their members for such purposes.

Bi-weekly intensive training programs and the one-year certificate course are readily available in Bronx, New York, and other regions based on request. If you are interested in hosting any of these programs in your region or country or church or ministry, please contact us. See details of our contact information and website on the back page.

## About the School of Deliverance

The School of Deliverance is an institution for training leaders, individuals, and church groups on how to minister deliverance. It is a practical training course where people are taught to minister to self, family members, friends, and church or fellowship members. In the process of training, people are also taught to be equipped for ministration and to face the battle of life as it is in the ministry.

The areas of study are in four modules. The first module focuses on how to minister deliverance; the second is on how to pull down satanic strongholds; the third module is on how to maintain your deliverance; and the fourth module is on the techniques of ministrations.

The School of Deliverance is organized and held in different parts of the world at various times. At seminar levels, one week or two weeks of intensive training are organized to help leaders and ministers or church or fellowship groups to establish a deliverance ministry or equip their members for such purposes.

Intensive training and a one-year certificate course is readily available in Bronx, New York, and other regions based on request. If you are interested in hosting the School of Deliverance in your region or country or church or ministry, please contact us. See details of our contact information and website on the back page.

# ABOUT THE AUTHOR

PAULINE WALLEY-DANIELS PHD is an ordained prophet-evangelist who teaches the Word of God with dramatic demonstrations. She is anointed by the Holy Spirit to teach the gospel of healing and deliverance and to impart the message of love and joy to the people.

Dr. Pauline travels to various parts of the world, ministering in churches, crusades, revivals, and seminars in various academic institutions, as well as speaking to professional bodies. She is also talented in writing, drama, poetry, and composing songs. Some of her musical works are also recorded. She is the author of sixteen other books.

Dr. Pauline is the President of Pauline Walley Evangelistic Ministries and Christian Communications as well the Director of the School of Intensive Training for Leadership Equipment that includes the School of Deliverance in New York. The School trains ministers, groups, and individuals all over the world. She is also an affiliate of Christian International Ministries Network and the

Vice President of North American Ministers Conference International.

Dr. Pauline Walley holds a Masters degree in Journalism, and her PhD in Pulpit Communications and Expository Preaching. She is married to Rev. Frederick Daniels of Overcomers Christian Center in New York.

**Contact Information**

- West Africa

Pauline Walley School of Deliverance
P.O. Box MS 301, Mile-Seven
Accra, Ghana.
Phone/Fax: (233) 403063 or 404184

- United Kingdom

Pauline Walley Christian Communications
P.O. Box 4673
London SE1 4UQ.
Phone: (44) 794-769-7867

- United States

Pauline Walley Christian Communications
P. O. Box 250
Bronx, NY 10467
Phone: (718) 652-2916
Fax: (718) 405-2035

**Email**: drpauline@paulinewalley.org